BOOKS BY WALDEMAR A. NIELSEN

AFRICA 1965
AFRICAN BATTLELINE 1965

AFRICA

A NEW YORK TIMES BYLINE BOOK

SOUTHEAST ASIA by TILLMAN DURDIN

AFRICA by WALDEMAR A. NIELSEN

RUSSIA by HARRISON E. SALISBURY

CHINA by HARRY SCHWARTZ

LATIN AMERICA by TAD SZULC

THE MIDDLE EAST by JAY WALZ

NEW YORK TIMES BYLINE BOOKS

AFRICA

by Waldemar A. Nielsen

A NEW YORK TIMES BYLINE BOOK

ATHENEUM

NEW YORK

1966

Copyright © 1965 by The New York Times Company
All rights reserved
Library of Congress catalog card number 65–27530
Published simultaneously in Canada by McClelland and Stewart Ltd.
Manufactured in the United States of America
Composition by H. Wolff, New York
Printed by The Murray Printing Company,
Forge Village, Massachusetts
Designed by Harry Ford
First Printing December 1965
Second Printing December 1966

TO MARCIA

CONTENTS

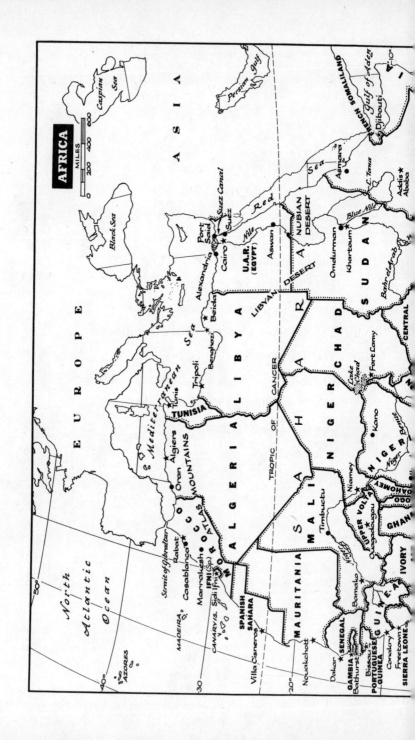

AFRICA

A NEW YORK TIMES BYLINE BOOK

I

The Rebirth of a Continent

ONLY A LITTLE MORE than a century ago white men penetrated the last unexplored region of Africa, around Lake Victoria, and solved the two-thousand-year-old mystery of the source of the Nile River. Westward of the immense lake stretched the Mountains of the Moon, on whose flanks roamed the last troupes of the Great Apes. In a town to the south, Ujiji, the American adventurer Henry Stanley found the dying Dr. Livingstone, an incident which thrilled the world and became the most widely known single event in the history of African exploration. One of the local tribal chiefs kept an extraordinary harem of wives who were force-fed like the pâté-de-fois-gras geese of Périgord until they were so fat they could not stand upright and instead groveled like seals about the straw mats of their huts.

In this same region, just a few years ago, a championship soccer game was played between the now independent countries of Uganda and Kenya. Several thousand spectators were in the modern stadium, having arrived by bus, motor scooter, automobile and bicycle, traveling on the broad boulevards of the capital city, Kampala. And between halves of the game a group of young students carried banners down the field soliciting contributions for Hungarian refugee relief.

That is Africa today—a continent of change and of contrast; of tiny villages lost in the bush and of new cities gleaming with skyscrapers; of timeless places and customs and of transistor radios bringing the latest world news to the most remote huts. This is the Africa of hope and of violence, of promise and of danger.

The Egyptians in 2500 B.C. were familiar with the northern part of Africa; Greek travelers in the third century B.C. visited deep in the interior; and the Egyptian scholar Ptolemy in the second century A.D. was able to produce a remarkably accurate map of many parts of the continent. In the eighth and ninth centuries Arab writers told of wonderful kingdoms rich with gold south of the Sahara. But for Americans, Africa has remained largely unknown and undiscovered to this day.

I remember making preparations a few years ago for my first trip to Africa. The month was July and I carefully packed my lightest clothes, afraid that even these would be too heavy for the fierce heat I expected. I was bound for Nairobi, the capital of Kenya, a city that sits virtually astride the equator.

Loaded with inoculations, anxieties and no small sense of adventure, I took off by airplane from New York ready for the steaming jungle, the crocodiles and the sheer "primitivism" of Africa.

But it seemed curiously cool when I reached my destination. And the car that met me at the airport passed through lovely rolling countryside as we sped along a broad new highway. We stopped finally at a modern hotel a few miles north of the city. Where was the heat? Where was the jungle?

In the following days I sat with a group of impressive young Africans discussing complex economic and constitutional questions. And in the evenings—in the chilling evenings—sitting before a roaring fire with a blanket from the bed around my shoulders I had time to reflect about my ignorance, and that of most of my countrymen, regarding the realities of Africa.

To our American great-grandfathers, Africa was little more than occasional tales of explorers, slave raids and elephant ivory. To our grandfathers, it was a vague awareness of brave missionaries, big-game hunts and Teddy Roosevelt's trophies. To our fathers, it was Tarzan stories and Humphrey Bogart movies.

But today Africa has become a drum-beat on our daily consciousness. News reports tell of rebellion and savage struggle in countries whose very names are unfamiliar—where the guns are said to come from Communist China and the aircraft from the United States. Great dams are constructed across rivers we have never heard of to irrigate unknown areas as large as whole regions of Europe. Black men with musical names and flowing robes move prominently across the international stage and we are reminded that a third of the members of the United Nations are African states, able by their votes to alter your future and mine and, indeed, the world's. And certainly recent American history has been affected by Africa—American Negroes are awakening with Africa to a new consciousness of their heritage.

Out of Africa comes a growing thunder of events —bizarre, dangerous, wonderful—and it is hard to put all that is happening into perspective. We know that Africa today is the most illiterate continent on earth, the most diverse, the most fragmented, the most diseased, not quite the most impoverished, but politically the most inexperienced. Why should this poor and weak area loom so importantly in our lives and our future? Why should Chinese guns in the hands of Africans be shooting at American planes flown by Cuban refugees near the border of a place called Uganda? Why is an American missionary doctor killed with screaming hatred by rebels in the Congo? What is the meaning of Africa for our lives in America—and for the peace of the world?

And in the light of all this turmoil and danger, why is there a sudden and growing movement of young Americans to Africa? Hundreds of them from our churches and universities are teaching in schools and working in hospitals there. Every summer more hundreds of American college students spend their vacations in Africa, laboring alongside young Africans to build schools, lay roads, dig wells —and talking together for long hours in the evening about the new Africa and the future. Some three thousand Peace Corps volunteers are at work, too, showing Africans a friendly, idealistic face of America rarely seen before on that continent, and their number grows each month.

For these young Americans, Africa has somehow become a symbol of the hopes and hazards of a changing world. Here, they feel, are all the intertwined problems of poverty, race and nation-building—and a place where with their own hands they can help do something about them. For their parents, the sinister and engrossing conflict in the world was between East and West. But younger Americans sense that for their generation the great danger to peace may be the division of the world between the colored nations and the white—which also happen to be the poor nations and the rich.

Such interest by Americans in Africa is new. But independent Africa is itself new. In 1954 a major study sponsored by the eminent Brookings Institution in Washington concluded: "With most of Africa still under colonial rule, the United States has few responsibilities there, nor is the region one of rapidly developing crises." Within three years of that prediction, crisis was piling upon crisis, the United States had become involved in rapidly growing responsibilities, and the political skyline of the African continent had become unrecognizable.

In the short span of one generation—from 1945 to 1965—some 225 million people in an area more than three times as large as the United States had taken—or had been granted—control of their own political destiny. The number of independent African-ruled states in Africa now totals 36, and of these only four existed as independent nations in 1955.

And so these middle years of the nineteen-sixties are a time of fresh beginning for the battered and backward continent. But it is also a time of danger, for the new nations born in the sudden onrush of independence are at the same time as frail as kittens —and as explosive as heat lightning.

II

The Legacy of Colonialism

AFRICA'S DIFFICULTIES did not begin with the arrival of the white man on the continent. But it is clear that his presence in the course of more than four centuries made certain problems immeasurably worse.

The practice of slavery, for example, was known in Africa from the earliest times, but it took on entirely new and destructive dimensions following that day in 1442 when a Portuguese naval officer returned 10 captured North Africans to their home and received as ransom a quantity of gold dust and 10 black slaves.

In the years thereafter Prince Henry the Navigator sent his mariners southward from Portugal along the African coast in quest of a new route to the riches of the Indies and for trade in gold, ivory and, increasingly, slaves.

What the European found in Africa at the time of the first incursions in the 15th century is a matter of argument. The chronicler of the Portuguese court in 1443 described the first group of African slaves to reach Lisbon in these words:

"They lived like beasts without any of the customs of rational creatures, since they did not know what were bread and wine, nor garments of cloth, nor life in the shelter of a home; and worse was their ignorance, which deprived them of all knowledge of good and permitted them only a life of brutish idleness."

There is growing evidence of a very different side to the picture—and that great kingdoms and a high level of civilization existed at various times and at different ages of history in Africa. Consider the testimony of an eminent German scholar, Leo Frobenius, who made about a dozen expeditions to various parts of Africa and was an authority on early societies:

"When they [the European navigators] arrived at Vaida in the gulf of Guinea, the captains were greatly astonished to find streets well laid out, bordered on either side for several leagues with two rows of trees; for days they traveled through a country of magnificent fields, inhabited by men clad in richly colored garments of their own weaving! Further south in the kingdom of the Congo, a swarming crowd dressed in silk and velvet . . . great States well-ordered, and down to the most minute details; powerful rulers; flourishing industries; civilized to the marrow of their bones. And the condition of the countries on the Eastern coast—Mozambique, for instance—was quite the same."

Whatever the condition of Africa at the time of the white man's arrival, however, there is no doubt about what followed. European slavers bled the continent down its western side while Arab slavers ravaged it on the east. By the 16th century the European plantations in North America and South America had a ravenous and growing need for cheap labor; before the end of that century of exploration and colonization almost two million Africans were seized, herded into slave ships and taken across the Atlantic. Of these, 900,000 arrived alive. In the 17th century three million slaves arrived; in the 18th century more than seven million; and in the 19th century, before the traffic was finally suppressed, another four million. Uncounted millions more died in bloody slave raids in Africa and in the filthy holds of Dutch, British, Portuguese, French and American ships into which they were packed like logs for transport to the New World. The effects on African tribes and kingdoms of this massive loss of generation after generation of their best manpower can only be imagined. Even worse was the havoc wrought by the wars and raids aided and encouraged by the slavers—wars that set African tribe against tribe and created marauding bands of thugs in the employ of the slavers who destroyed any sense of peace or security in the countryside.

With the merchants, the slavers, the soldiers and the settlers came missionaries. They brought many benefits to the Africans in the form of education and medical services; but the missionary record in Africa is a mixed one. For every selfless and devoted man or woman of the church there was another who participated actively in the slave trade, who cooperated with the most exploitive of the colonial governments or who resisted first the advancement and later the independence of the African. And nearly all the missionaries, the kind as well as the cruel, helped create a feeling on the part of the African that he was sinful in his natural ways, wrong in his beliefs and inferior in his abilities.

Almost as soon as the slave trade was ended in the 19th century, the countries of Europe inflicted a new calamity upon Africa. Until then only patches of African territory near the coasts had been occupied. But in the last decades of the century the general control of Africa by France, Britain and Portugal was disturbed by the entry of Belgium under King Leopold II and Germany under Bismarck, both of whom moved to lay claim to colonies. Suddenly, in an atmosphere of mutual suspicion and distrust, the countries of Europe began a scramble for the unclaimed portions of Africa, bickering and bargaining with one another over disputed areas.

This strange state of international cupidity came to a climax during the Conference of Berlin in 1885, when the European powers sliced up the entire continent and allocated its parts to themselves. The lines on the map which even today mark off the countries of Africa were largely drawn by these European statesmen sitting in ornate European conference rooms. Here, a line was drawn due north simply because an old slaving station and fortress was located at that point on an African coast. There, two European powers each claimed a particular area; they compromised, split the difference and drew a frontier without reference to the tribal, linguistic or even geographical realities of Africa.

All was not static after this Conference, of course. Following World War I Germany lost her African possessions to the victors. And throughout the continent scattered stirrings of African demands for independence could be detected, as well as a glimmering awareness on the part of the colonial powers of a need to do something for the lot of the people. But it was World War II that marked the turning point for the long-dominated Dark Continent.

Tens of thousands of Africans served with the Allied forces as support and combat troops and were thereby exposed to the ideas and ideals as well as the sacrifices of the war. Many returned home to various parts of Africa demanding their political rights with new aggressiveness. They wanted the Four Freedoms proclaimed by President Franklin Roosevelt—freedom of speech and worship, freedom from want and fear—plus a fifth freedom of their own, freedom from colonial control.

Their political movements were weak and they had neither arms nor finances in any quantity. But they were able to prevail over the great European countries in large part for the same reason that the small forces of General Washington had been able to prevail over the armies of England—namely, their powerful adversaries were at the moment weakened and preoccupied with other problems.

World War II, which radically changed world power relationships, left Europe disrupted, divided and fearful. On the other hand, the strength of the United States had become pre-eminent; and the Soviet Union, although it had suffered great devastation, also emerged as a vastly greater influence on the world scene.

Despite the Soviet Union's own colonial control of the countries of Eastern Europe (Hungary, Czechoslovakia, Poland, Rumania and the other "satellites"), the Kremlin was determinedly opposed to Western European colonialism. The tough and cynical Stalin saw the world as a battleground and all strangers (even former allies) as enemies. "The backs of the British will be broken not on the River Thames, but on the Yangtze, the Ganges and the Nile," he had once said. Consequently, once the Nazis had been defeated, he turned his attention to European control in Asia and Africa and by infiltration, subversion and propaganda attempted to undermine it.

Within the Western countries sentiment about empire was deeply divided. Winston Churchill had declared during the war (in connection with the Battle of Egypt) that he had "not become the King's First Minister to preside over the liquidation of the British Empire." But in fact many of his countrymen as well as Europeans generally had come to realize that they had vastly overestimated the economic value of the colonies. Moreover, ideas of democracy and human rights had so penetrated European life during the first half of the 20th century that the political foundations of colonialism had largely rotted away.

Thus, Europe after 1945 had less enthusiasm than before for empire and she found her position in Africa as in Asia beleaguered on all sides—by the African and Asian leaders, by the Soviet Union and in a subtle and indirect way by the generally anti-colonial viewpoint of the United States. Lacking both the firm will and the resources to resist these multiple pressures, the European colonial powers gave way.

In a vast historical transformation, independence for Africa swept through the North and the arid Saharan reaches, the region of the tropical rain forests and the handsome highlands of East and Central Africa.

For most African countries independence was won by political agitation and negotiation, not bloodshed. The colonial powers generally withdrew without having attempted to subdue the African nationalists by massive armed force. Consequently, the triumphant ceremony in each new nation when the European flag was hauled down for the last time generally took place in an atmosphere of good feeling.

But in a few places, notably Algeria, independence came only after years of hard fighting—in the course of which both sides ultimately resorted to methods of torture and barbarity which left an enduring residue of resentment.

The record of the colonial powers is equally varied as regards their contributions to African advancement during their period of control. Once they finally abandoned their huge traffic in slavery some of them provided admirable instances of support for education, for economic development and for preparation of the African for self-government. But others to this day—through their governing practices, their racial policies and their greed—bear with crushing weight upon the black man.

The Congo after 80 years of Belgian rule came to independence with 12 African university graduates in the entire country. Several African countries at the end of colonialism were left with only the most meager structure of medical services and secondary schools. Even the manner of the final departure of the European colonial administrators was sometimes most ungraceful. The French, for example, when they had to leave Guinea, ripped the telephones off the walls and smashed all the light fixtures. Guinea, alone among other territories previously held by the French, had elected to cut all her ties with France. It is said that French fury was so great that they even destroyed all the prison records; Guinean officials afterward had to ask each prisoner what offense he had committed and how long a sentence he was serving.

Therefore, in some countries the legacy of colonialism was blood and bitterness; but in most the foundations of friendship as well as independence were well set down.

The ending of colonialism changed the political reality of Africa—but beneath the crazy-quilt borders of that new reality lies a deeper reality—the reality of the declining but still dominant tribal pattern of African life. Far older than the new nation-states and older even than colonialism are the traditional groupings of Africans speaking the same language, sharing the same beliefs and traditions, and feeling the same loyalties. In much of Africa many people still feel more deeply attached to their tribe than to their nation, a fact which has important implications.

III

The Tribes—Roadblocks or Building Blocks?

NOT LONG AGO—reported a *New York Times* correspondent, Lloyd Garrison, from a newly independent West African nation, Cameroon—the European manager of a branch airline office reluctantly discharged his booking clerk, an African Negro. "I had no choice," the manager said.

He had employed two Negroes: a counter clerk to take reservations and a booking clerk to send messages confirming the reservations. When they were hired the manager had no idea they were from hostile tribes.

"The booking clerk sent the cables all right," the manager said, "but they were all for the wrong flights. It was a deliberate attempt to sabotage his tribal rival."

According to the manager, both men were efficient and well educated—"emancipated Africans." "If tribalism comes before professionalism with people like this," he asked, "what is this country's future?"

Cameroon, like most African states, is made up of many and diverse elements: one part speaks English, the other French. A large part of the population is Moslem; another large part Christian. In all there are 129 tribes and linguistic groups in the country. Throughout Africa it is estimated that there are nearly 1,000 different tribal and language groups, made up of individuals of marvelously varied size, color and appearance—from the masked Tuaregs and white Berbers of the North to the true Negroes in the center to the timid Bushmen and the golden Hottentots in the South. There is no "typical" African.

Some of the tribes could well be called nations—for example, the Yoruba of Western Nigeria, which includes several millions of people and represents an admirable tradition of cultural and intellectual achievement. But many of the tribes are small and backward, fortresses of primitivism and the past.

For the individual members tribal relations can be a precious comfort: among all the disintegrative modernizing forces with which the African now has to contend, the tribe may be the base of his sense of identity and stability. But for the new African nations, tribal divisions can be serious obstacles to progress and to unity.

I vividly recall a sight a few years ago at an East African airport, a regular stop for transcontinental jets. Standing on the observation deck of the modern terminal building that day were two solemn warriors of a tribe known as the Masai. The men were tall, lean and muscular; each wore his hair in an elaborate coiffure, carried a dark woolen cape over his shoulder and held a spear in his hand. They stood side by side, erect and proud, watching the great aluminum machines arrive and depart.

One could wonder what thoughts lay behind their steady and intent gaze—but it would be a serious mistake to assume that, having glimpsed the mechanical marvels of the jet age, they were ready to drop their spears and customs and adopt our mode of living. The Masai are an old and mighty tribe whose members have a rigorous code of courage, and they are held in high regard, even awe, by many others in their area. Their tribal life is complex and each man's life is interwoven with it. They consider themselves the bearers of a long and noble tradition.

Nonetheless, the pressures of change are being felt. The Masai supported the drive for independence of their country. Many of the young men and some of the young women now seek education. But the process of changing the Masai and the members of many other tribes of Africa into urban, industrialized people will be long and hard. Even more difficult will be the task of evolving patterns of change that will reconcile the values and virtues of traditional Africa with the material and other benefits of Western civilization.

Everywhere in Africa today the new lives with and is superimposed on the old, and the importance of both must be comprehended. And for every African the process of change is a personal drama, sometimes exciting, more often bewildering and painful.

In the middle of Africa, in the area of the Copperbelt, a widely read newspaper is the *Central African Mail*. It carries a daily "advice to the lovelorn" column which brings an unending stream of letters from the remote bush country, small mining towns and modern cities. The letters give a clear and often poignant picture of the everyday life of the African and of the effect of historic change on the individual person.

The importance of the tribe even to an educated man is visible in this inquiry:

My uncle, who is village headman and much respected, has written telling me he has found a wife and I must hurry home for marriage. She is a little girl of 13 and has had no schooling. I am a graduate and have warm feeling towards a lady teacher in my town. But my uncle says he will be disgraced if I do not follow his wishes and is adamant about this child who is unknown to me.

The problem of conflicting values and customs is reflected in this one:

I love two girls. My mother likes them and wants me to marry them both. She says she will pay their *lobola* [dowry or bride-price]. I am a Christian and the Bible says you must only have one wife. But it also says I must obey my parents.

And Josephine, the columnist who answers these inquiries, replied:

When to obey a parent means you will commit a sin, you must put the Church's teaching first. Polygamy does not often bring a happy life. It is unlikely that the two wives will live peaceably together, and it is a costly business as you have two of them to feed and clothe.

Marriage across tribal lines can also produce problems: Thus:

I recently married Miss Right, and have no objection to continued matrimony till death us do part, but one problem hurts us. This is our £35 radio. Being of different tribe from my wife, I do not know what to do every afternoon at four when the studio broadcasts in vernaculars. She calls for one tongue, I for another. What shall we do? Must we remain without a radio?

Josephine answered:

One day she listens to the radio while you read the newspaper. Next day you listen while she reads the newspaper.

Even politics can confuse romance in changing Africa:

The parents of my girl belong to African National Congress. I am 25 and madly in love with her, but when I ask their consent they refuse because I belong to the United National Independence Party. The father will not consider my proposal unless I join [the African National] Congress and I do not want to do this. Nor do I want to miss my lovely girl.

Tribal problems and the fusing of small groups into larger political units have of course been characteristic of the process of nation-building throughout history. Julius Caesar wrote of the problem of subjugating the various French, German, Italian and British tribes which became part of the Roman Empire. It was not until relatively recent times that the power of the local barons was broken and

France became a single nation. Even today a Scotsman will argue about whether the fiercely independent tribes of the Highlands have been absorbed into what is called Britain; and Belgium is split in a bitter and permanent "tribal" struggle between the Flemings and the Walloons.

In Africa a multitude of new forces—nationalism, nationhood, industrialization, urbanization, education—are simultaneously at work to dissolve and modify old tribal patterns and to develop new and larger patterns of loyalty and attachment.

But the problem of overcoming tribal fragmentation and conflict will be especially difficult because of the bizarre network of national boundaries which the new governments have inherited from their colonial past. Some of the "nations" which resulted are mere remnants of territory and a few people, with no chance to survive as self-supporting countries. One new nation, Gambia, is a bit of land as wide as a river delta and as long as a 19th-century steamboat could navigate upstream.

The Ewe tribe in West Africa finds that part of its people now live in a country called Togo and the rest in one called Ghana. The Ewe have existed as a tribe for centuries; Togo and Ghana are recent political inventions. The Bakongo tribe now finds itself partly in Angola and partly in the two Congo Republics (the former Belgian Congo and the former French Congo). The Somali tribe finds itself partly in Somalia, partly in French Somaliland, partly in Ethiopia and partly in northern Kenya.

Thus many of the new African nations have built-in potential border disputes with their neighbors and subdivided populations. In time, if common sense prevails, there will have to be adjustments of frontiers and hopefully some regrouping and consolidation of the smaller, non-viable countries. But if Africans behave as most of humanity has behaved in dealing with such problems in the past, common sense will succumb in too many cases to political ambition, pride and conflict.

Serious as the frictions between African countries may be, the main tensions in Africa are nevertheless within each country. These are in large part the result of different rates of change: between the rapidity of political change and the agonizing slowness of social change; between the rapid impact of modern medicine in reducing death rates and the slow process of lowering birth rates; between the rapid increase of the expectations of people for material progress and the slow process of increasing productivity; between the rapid influx of young people into the mushrooming cities and the slow course of increasing the number of industrial jobs for them; between the rapidity with which political rights can be given and the slowness with which political experience and responsibility develop.

In the gaps between these differing rates of

change lie dangers and difficulties. These internal strains, plus the legacy of backwardness and fragmentation which Africa inherits from the past, explain the frailty of these new nations. Their emergence as independent countries opens up inspiring possibilities. But in their weakness there is also the eventuality of chaos and international peril. Thus this whole vast changing continent is tremblingly poised on the razor's edge between peace and calamity.

IV

The Pressures of Poverty

AN AMERICAN BOY who reaches 16 has lived about one-quarter of his life, statistically speaking. He has almost certainly completed grade school, will probably finish high school and—if he so wishes—has a fair chance of graduating from college. In most cases he eats regularly and amply, has adequate clothing and, when he occasionally falls ill, has the benefit of modern medicines and professional medical care. His life is served by a multitude of machines. The heavy lifting, digging and moving is done by motors and engines. Trains, automobiles and airplanes take him effortlessly from place to place. He has at his disposal dozens of technical devices and conveniences, from electric lights to the telephone and television. He is probably an urban person accustomed to the ways of the city, unfamiliar with the farm and even less with the forest.

In contrast, an African boy of the same age has lived nearly half his life, statistically speaking. It is unlikely that he can read or write or that he has finished primary school. There is only slight chance that he will enter or finish high school and less than one chance in a thousand that he will be able to enter college. His diet, even when sufficient in quantity, is starchy and seriously deficient in vitamins and protein. He will probably be stricken by serious disease in the course of his life, and in that event it is unlikely that he will have access to medicines, a doctor or a hospital. His life has only been touched by the industrial age—he has listened to a radio, has seen an automobile and has probably watched an airplane fly overhead. His hope is to have a bicycle; to have his own car would be too wild a dream. To him the farm and the forest are close and familiar; the city is strange and distant.

An American teacher in Uganda, Mr. Peter Buttenwieser, showed his ninth-grade class a large picture of New York City. These were some of the questions they asked:

"What do the people cultivate in this city? And where?"

"Do the people take their automobiles up to their apartments with them?"

"Don't people get tired walking up so many steps each day?"

And then this comment:

"It must be frightening when the wind blows and all the buildings start swaying back and forth!"

One way to measure the contrast between the African's life and our own would be to say that an American family can hardly crowd its belongings into a moving van, but most African families can easily carry their possessions in a hand basket. Another way would be to say that the average income of an African is about 40 cents a day. Such poverty is one of the problems that will trouble the world and endanger the peace for the remainder of the century—for at least two-thirds of humanity subsist at the same level as the African—and many are in actual misery.

The African is poor because his methods of production are backward and inefficient. The rewards of his labor, no matter how exhausting his primitive efforts may be, are small.

A few Africans make their living by fishing, by commerce or in the factory. But three out of every four Africans live as farmers or herdsmen on the land —land that is enormously varied. Some of it is dank gloomy forest; some is shimmering savanna—grassy and wooded plains; and a considerable part is burning, idle desert. Some areas look like the broad open country of Colorado or the mountains of Wyoming;

the air sparkles, a man can see 100 miles and a blanket is welcome every night of the year. There are a few large and modern cities, but the vast majority of people live in scattered small towns and villages, often isolated and remote.

In these villages everybody works—not only the men and boys but also the women and girls and even the little children. The women are up before dawn, in the fields or the forest or at the well— cooking, gathering fuel, grinding grain into meal, caring for the sick.

The men and boys are occupied with clearing brush, tending the cattle, making fences, hunting and trapping. The tempo of life is slow. Personal relationships are warm, close, and with all the work there is endless talk: stories, argument, gossip and, among the elders, serious discussion—what the Africans call *palaver*.

As for all who live on the land, natural hazards are a constant threat: drought, flood and epidemic. For the cattleraiser there is the problem of the tsetse fly and tick-borne diseases that may annihilate his herds. For the farmer there are marauding animals, crop failures and physical accidents. Perhaps his most general problem is the poor quality of the African soil; in some localities it is thin and subject to erosion; in others its nutrients have been washed away by excessive rainfall. As a result, a common pattern is for the farmer, after the soil in a particular place is exhausted, to move to another. There he burns off the brush and starts the process over again. The wastefulness of this practice has been described by a former colonial officer who on many occasions saw "hundreds of miles of pasture land and light forest reduced to a blackened, smoking ruin, as the first step on the part of three or four men and their wives in the cultivation of maybe an acre each."

The people of the countryside generally eat or use what they produce and are largely self-sufficient. But increasingly they produce crops which they sell to merchants and which the merchants ultimately sell for export—coffee, cocoa, palm oil. With the proceeds they buy industrial goods they need. Their link with the outside world of commerce is a system of transportation and communication that inadequately combines much that is ancient with some that is modern. A few railroads vein the edges of the continent, built generally to haul ores and minerals from the inland mines to the coasts. A sparse and broken web of hard-surfaced roads exists; however, much freight moves along the many rivers that finger deep into the interior. The advent of aircraft has been a boon because of the vast distances that must be spanned, but air travel is for the few and the foreigner. For the African the most common means of travel is by foot or bicycle, and the moving of goods is still largely accomplished on the backs and heads of human beings, whose feet have beaten out of the bush the innumerable footpaths of the interior.

One hundred years ago not less than 500,000 caravan porters passed annually through the single Arab trading center of Tabora in Tanganyika, each carrying a load of 50 or 60 pounds. To this day most of the goods Africa sells and buys begin or end their journey carried by a man along a footpath— farm or plantation products going out, cooking pots, salt or a sewing machine coming in.

The African of the nineteen-sixties, therefore, still lives and works in much the same fashion as his forebears in centuries past. But there is one vital difference: today many are aware of their poverty. They know that misery is not the universal and inevitable lot of mankind. This new awareness—fed by radio broadcasts, newspapers, magazines, motion pictures, tourists from abroad, political propaganda and young people who have acquired education and have seen other parts of the world—has produced a demand for change and a dangerous but understandable impatience.

I have seen this determination and discontent in the eyes of villagers and city slum dwellers in Asia, the Middle East and the Caribbean as well as in Africa. I shall never forget the moment some years ago when an old man digging an irrigation ditch near a tropical town came up to me with great pride, opened his mouth and showed me his bare toothless gums. He had sold his farm to send his son to school

—and the gold in his teeth to pay for the boy's textbooks.

This restless desire for improvement governs the internal politics of every new African country. The joys of the moment of independence have been sweet for the people of Africa—but they rather quickly pass. And every African leader knows that to remain in power after the excitement of the flag-raising celebration is over he will sooner or later have to do something about jobs, education, wages, the prices of farm products and the conditions of life both in the countryside and in the cities.

Temporarily the people will wait; and for a short while lack of economic and social progress can be hidden by dramatic and distracting political maneuvers. But eventually, unless there is progress, there will be trouble—trouble for the people if their leaders try to suppress discontent by force, or for the leaders if the discontent can find expression.

Thus Africa is being driven toward progress and the overhauling of its ancient and unproductive ways by the force of human wants and needs. But, paradoxically, if people's hopes are the thrust behind the present movement forward, people's habits and fixed ideas are also the main obstacle to change and improvement. The discontented African, although determined to see his family free from the burden of want, is also a tangle of attitudes, beliefs and fears rooted in the past and extremely difficult to change.

Take the case of an African farmer scratching out a meager living on his thin soil. Even when he is shown modern and better methods he may be reluctant, even resistant, about trying them. This is not because he is by nature mulish or stupid; rather it is because he is operating in a situation in which there is no margin for error, no room for risky experiment. If he misses one crop, his family may starve. He knows that the practices of the past worked for his grandfather and father before him and he is willing to change only after a clear and convincing demonstration of the results of newer methods.

Or take his attitude toward the desirability of having numerous children. Throughout the world rapid population growth is a deadly enemy in the war against poverty. Modern drugs and pesticides when introduced in backward areas have dramatically reduced death rates and have thereby caused a sharp growth in population. Consequently, whatever increases in economic output have been achieved are promptly absorbed by the rapid increase in the number of people to be fed, housed and clothed.

Although DDT and vaccinations can reduce death rates almost immediately, the number of babies born per thousand people in any backward society is a figure extremely difficult to lower. Children, and especially sons, have come to be regarded over the centuries as an economic benefit, even to a poor family. With hard work to be done in fields or forest, extra sons mean extra hands to help. And for parents without any other form of social security, children mean reassurance and assistance in their old age. Children almost everywhere in the backward areas of the world have come to be a mark of prestige, a sign of the manhood of the father and the womanhood of the mother. In turn, these profound feelings have been reflected in and further solidified by religious beliefs and practices. Thus, to keep a baby from dying may require only a single injection, but persuading parents not to have a sixth or seventh child doomed to hardship and disease may require a painful and revolutionary change in their whole outlook on life.

Nor is the problem merely one of attitudes in the backward countries themselves. Until very recent years some of our leading American missionary groups and foundations forged ahead with medical programs in the poor countries without considering the consequences of their actions in terms of population growth. U. S. Government assistance programs went ahead with health and agricultural projects without being able, because of some Congressional and public opinion in the United States, to do anything about the population explosion that tended to result from their efforts.

The problem of controlling population growth lies at the heart of the task of breaking mankind out of the prison of poverty. But it cannot be solved by simply distributing birth-control pills. It involves a complex need for knowledge and changes in human beliefs and values.

Like every aspect of what is commonly called the problem of economic development, overpopulation is a problem of transforming human beings—their outlook, ideas, and institutions.

Even an economic problem that may sound purely technical—such as reducing the rapid turnover of African industrial labor—is basically a complicated matter of changing people's feelings, fears and aspirations.

Take, for example, the case of Stephen Chimano, who grew up in a village in Rhodesia where his parents, his grandparents, his uncles, aunts, cousins, brothers and sisters all lived closely together in a typically African "extended family." In that setting he was never without companionship, never without someone to talk to, never without someone to help or be helped by in case of need. In return he was subject to the confinement and the comfort of complex obligations to conform to the tribal rules, to help and share with the others of his family.

Then he moved to Bulawayo, a distant city, to take a factory job. He had to be trained, which took time and cost his employer a certain investment.

But, living in the city, Stephen was alone for the first time in his life and he was lonely—with a loneliness close to torture, a loneliness incomprehensible to those of us not brought up in an extended-family system.

He was also afraid in his loneliness. At home, if he was sick, if he needed food, if he needed any help, his relatives were there. But in the city there was no one who cared. Nor could he forget his responsibilities to his relatives in the village—to his parents, who were growing old, and to the youngsters who had to be initiated into the customs and traditions of the tribe. These obligations could not be fulfilled from afar, and he felt guilty and neglectful. In addition to all the rest, he simply could not adjust to the life of the city. The gap between what he had always known—the life of the hoe, the canoe, deer hunting and moral rectitude—and that of the conveyor belt, motor cars, selfishness and promiscuity in the city was simply too wide.

So about the time his training in the factory was complete—when Stephen had become an effective, productive worker and had saved a little money—he quit and returned home. For him it was a return to sanity—to the village, where "men are men and women are proud of them," where he could find a wife and bring up his children in an atmosphere without juvenile delinquency, prostitution, greed and selfishness. But from an economic viewpoint his return was a waste—a loss of the investment made in his training, a loss of skill and productivity, and a setback, however small, to the development of his country.

For every Stephen Chimano who returns to the village from the city there are a dozen who move to the attractions of the city from the drabness of the countryside. Both movements have their economic effects and both emphasize that the solution for most problems of economic development must be found in the mysterious regions of psychology, sociology and even moral values. In the end the problem of installing even the most complicated machine is far simpler than the task of changing the attitudes of a single man or the habits of a single village.

More and more, economists have come to recognize that changing human attitudes and developing human knowledge and skills are necessary first steps in economic development. It has been obvious for a long time that the natural resources of a country have little to do with its industrial progress or its standard of living. Japan and Switzerland are relatively poor in land and resources, but their progress has been rapid and their people are prosperous. The Congo is one of the richest areas of the earth, but its people are poor.

Yet it is only recently that spending large sums of money on education in the underdeveloped areas of the world has been recognized as an investment, not a luxury. Such investment should, in fact, be put high on the list of priorities in any effort to change a country's economic backwardness. Economists now estimate that, measured purely in money terms, the investment a country makes in educating and training its citizens pays off at something like 15 per cent a year in terms of increased national product. That is why foreign economic aid programs now give educational projects much greater emphasis.

One interesting result, in the case of Africa, has been the destruction of some old prejudices about the intellectual ability of the black man. Until a very few years ago the number of African students in American universities was tiny. But since the wave of independence in Africa in the late nineteen-fifties the number has grown rapidly. One of the principal scholarship programs for African students coming to the United States has been organized by 215 of our leading universities. To date, more than 1,000 carefully selected young Africans from most of the countries of the continent have been brought here under this program for four years of university work.

The number of drop-outs and academic failures has been almost infinitesimal. Moreover, the general average of their grades has been clearly better than the average for American students in the same schools, despite the fact that many of these young

Africans have had to overcome language difficulties and severe problems of social adjustment. The distribution of the grades of some 750 students studied in 1963-64 was: A's—23 per cent; B's—40 per cent; C's—29 per cent; D's—6 per cent; F's—2 per cent. Such evidence, if nothing else, should dispel any doubts about the determination of young Africans to acquire an education or about their intelligence and learning capacity.

American economic aid programs are now concentrating also on the improvement and expansion of schools and colleges in Africa. Not surprisingly, improvement has been slow, for great educational institutions are not created overnight, either in Africa or anywhere else. Some 250 years after the founding of Harvard University in the United States, one of its great presidents, Charles W. Eliot, tried to institute some much needed reforms. At that time the law and medical faculties at Harvard gave degrees to any man who had merely paid three semester bills covering 18 months and who had not been very irregular in attending lectures. Dr. Eliot in his autobiography, *A Late Harvest,* tells the following story: When I asked the medical faculty in 1870 if it would be possible to substitute an hour's written examination for the five minutes' oral examination [a five-minute interview with the professor of each of the nine principal subjects then taught in the school] for graduation, the answer came promptly from the Head of the Faculty: 'Written examinations are impossible in the Medical School. A majority of the students cannot write well enough.' "

New technical training centers and universities are mushrooming all over Africa and are developing vigorously. But time and patience will be necessary. The training of men and the building of human institutions produce a rich harvest—but only after a slow ripening.

Despite all the problems with which Africa must contend—the poverty, the lack of transportation, the population explosion, the disease, the malnutrition, the primitive habits and work techniques, the lag in technical education—slow progress is being made. Yet the persistent question that must be asked is whether improvement is coming at a sufficient rate to satisfy aspirations, dampen discontent and head off political pressures which are building up.

The economic goals the African countries have set for themselves are at the same time ambitious and yet pathetically low. In general, Africa hopes to raise per-capita annual income from $134 in 1963 to $178 in 1973. This is what economists would call a rate of sustained growth of 5 per cent a year.

When you compare what Africans *hope* to achieve by 1973 with what the United States and the countries of Western Europe are *likely* to achieve in the same period, a startling fact becomes apparent:

the gap between the rich countries and the poor will become steadily wider, not narrower. Per-capita income in the United States by 1973 will probably have increased from $2,400 a year to $2,589 a year, and in Western Europe from $1,000 to $1,194. All this while the Africans hope to raise their per-capita income over these 10 years by $44, or from a daily income of 37 cents in 1963 to a level of 48 cents a day by 1973.

Note that even if Africa achieves its goals, the gap between incomes in Africa and the developed areas will *increase, not decrease,* over the decade. Between Africa and Europe the spread at the beginning of the period was $866. But at the end it will be $1,016. At the beginning of the period the spread between per-capita income in Africa and the United States was $2,266; at the end of the decade it will be $2,411.

As President Julius Nyerere of Tanzania has said, "For all the consciousness of world economic inequality, for all the international organizations which have been established to remedy the situation, the gap between the haves and the have-nots is widening on a progressive scale."

Will an increase in annual income for each African—if it is achieved—from $134 in 1963 to $178 in 1973 be enough to satisfy his burning hopes and ease his discontent?

Does the widening gap between the rich and the

poor countries spell a world crisis in the brewing?

The race is against time and disorder—and the clock ticks on.

	Per-Capita Income 1963 (Dollars)	Growth Rate of Gross Domestic Product (Per Cent)	Growth Rate of Population (Per Cent)	Growth Rate of Per-Capita Income (Per Cent)	Per-Capita Income 1973 (Dollars)
United States	2,400	2.5	1.7	0.8	2,589
West. Europe	1,000	3.5	0.7	2.8	1,194
Africa	134	5.0	2.1	2.9	178

V

The Prospects for Progress

"Your American businessmen are the most timid. The ones we see here are interested only in two kinds of projects—'fast buck' operations, as you call them, such as the buying of diamonds or timber for quick resale. Or the traditional kinds of investment—oil or mining. What we need most—new factories—they are afraid of."

These were the words of a young African official now in charge of economic development in his country. He was talking to me bluntly as an old friend. In taking notes on what he said, I promised not to reveal his identity so that he need not hold back critical or undiplomatic opinions. Through the eyes and from the perspective of such a man many aspects of African development take on a very different and much more realistic appearance.

"Why is this?" I asked, referring to his statement about American businessmen.

Mr. X.: "Maybe it's because they are inexperienced in Africa. But I get the feeling they are also very panicky. The smallest newspaper report of a tribal fight in the bush and the Americans want to grab their money and run for home."

Nielsen: "Let's come back to that later. First, let's talk about fundamentals: Is there really any chance of Africa's becoming a prosperous, developed area?"

Mr. X.: "Believe me, we have problems galore. But never forget that Africa has richer possibilities than any of the other so-called backward areas. We have water power for all the electricity we will ever need. We have the greatest forests on earth. We have the richest storehouse of minerals—from gold to cobalt to iron ore. And we have enough land to feed half of humanity.

"Sometimes, when I look at Africa from an airplane window, I think of how it must have been once in your Far West. . . . Railroads will have to be built, people trained and a lot of research done about our soils. These things will be difficult. But the possibilities are there.

"If we can find men and ideas—big enough ideas —this continent will someday bloom and be one of the glories of the world."

NIELSEN: "What is your plan, your strategy, for bringing these dreams to reality?"

MR. X.: "That's a big word—'plan.' You can't have a plan without information and we lack a lot of the essential information you take for granted. So call it a common-sense approach—a strategy if you like, but a rather rough and ready one. First, I think we have to do something to improve agriculture, because that is how three-fourths of our people earn their living. We have to encourage them to produce crops that can be sold for cash in world markets. This means more training for our farmers. And we'll have to give them more low-interest loans for seed and equipment along with a great deal of encouragement.

"Second, we have to do something to develop Africans qualified in management, manufacturing and commerce. Our people have very little commercial or business experience and it will take a long time to develop a capable group of African entrepreneurs and managers. Nevertheless, until we get a substantial number of such people, we can only remain at an economic disadvantage.

"You know, to hear some economists talk, you might think that the problem of development could be solved like an algebraic equation. But one of our problems in Africa is that what the world knows about economics—and it isn't much, really—has largely been developed by economists in Western countries working on the kinds of problems you find in your advanced countries. We have yet to produce a group of African economists to analyze our economic problems in terms of actual African conditions. Until the day when there is a true African branch of economists we will have to rely considerably on the best guesses of noneconomists like me."

NIELSEN: "You talk about agriculture. But hasn't there been a tendency for some African countries to want a steel mill or a hydroelectric dam in preference to practical agricultural projects?"

MR. X.: "That is true, to a degree. But don't forget that there has been considerable pressure from the foreign aid agencies in the direction of big projects—dams, railroads and so on—in preference to unspectacular little projects for the farmer in the back country. I think on balance there has been as much fondness for 'showcase' projects on the part of the foreigners as on the part of the African."

NIELSEN: "You keep mentioning aid from abroad. Is this essential to your development plan? What about self-help?"

MR. X.: "There is a great deal we can and should do—and *are* doing—for ourselves. But we are starting from a very low level. Therefore we are going to have to rely heavily on foreign investment and foreign aid. We need bulldozers and tractors and machinery, and the only place we can get them is abroad—for cash which we don't have. Practically no African country has a development plan which doesn't depend on outside funds for at least 20 per cent of its requirements, and quite a few look to foreign assistance to cover more than half of their needs.

"In an African country if you have copper mines, for example, or if you produce cocoa for the world market, you can tax such products at the port of exit. In that way you get some of the money you need to run the government and to finance your development plan. But on the whole there is little possibility of taxing the general population or looking to private savings for capital needs. Our people are simply too poor to be taxable. And they have too little beyond their daily subsistence requirements to be able to save. Fundamentally, that is why we must look abroad for much of our basic financing."

NIELSEN: "As you see it, what are your chances of getting the capital you need from foreign private investors?"

MR. X.: "We have some hope in this direction, but not much. The British and the French have long experience in Africa and they will be an important source of investment. The Germans are increasingly interested in Africa and so are the Italians. And the Israelis have financed some very good things.

"To get back to your American businessmen for a moment, I suppose another reason they take little interest in investment in agriculture or manufacturing in Africa is that they have such good investment possibilities in the States.

"But there is still this fact of their timidity—of their tendency to flee at the first sign of trouble. What amuses me is that as soon as there is trouble other foreign investors, such as the Greeks, the Lebanese and the Germans, tend to move in with the hope of buying up properties at bargain prices.

"However, in recent months, I think, there has been a growth of American interest in African investment. I hope so, because the more investment you have here, the better for us—and the more interest you will take in Africa generally."

NIELSEN: "How much foreign aid in contrast to private investment are you receiving? And has it been useful?"

MR. X.: "Let me try to put the whole matter of foreign aid in perspective—in African perspective, that is.

"To begin with, the big source of economic aid to Africa is not the United States but Western Europe. We get more than twice the help from Europe that we get from your country."

NIELSEN: "What about aid from international organizations—like United Nations technical assistance?"

MR. X.: "This is extremely important, especially because the U.N. programs are intelligently directed and because the personnel they hire are very capable. But in dollar quantity it is very small. I wish it were much larger."

NIELSEN: "What about the Communist countries?"

MR. X.: "Both the Russians and the Chinese have made large promises and noisy propaganda— but in fact they have delivered extremely little. However, Communist interest in Africa, both from the Russian and the Chinese side, seems to be growing very rapidly. Communist aid practically doubled from 1962 to 1964."

NIELSEN: "How would you compare the Chinese and Russian aid programs?"

MR. X.: "The Russians act like tough and inept big businessmen; they drive a hard bargain when they offer assistance, and in the end the prices they charge for their supplies and technicians are very high.

"But little of their technique and equipment is well suited to African conditions. Also, I have the impression that the Russian doesn't find it easy to get along with the African. I know that the African finds it very difficult to get along with the Russian.

"I would judge that the Russians feel that most of their African aid projects have turned out rather badly. From the African side, Russian economic help is about the least desirable and useful of any that we have received."

NIELSEN: "How about the Chinese?"

MR. X.: "The Chinese are very different from the Russians. They have a better sense of the kind of projects and the kind of help needed in Africa. The projects they have started have been, on the whole, well chosen and well executed.

"However, on the political side, the Chinese get involved with every group of troublemakers they can find, and they are lavish in their bribery.

"I would say that, in general, we are very distrustful of the Chinese—even though we may have to turn to them in certain cases for some kinds of military or political help your Western countries refuse to provide."

NIELSEN: "The Chinese make a great point in their propaganda about the fact that they, like the African, are nonwhite. Is this racial argument effective with Africans?"

MR. X.: "Yes, they refer to this constantly—but I think the African finds at least as much difference between himself and the Chinese as he does between himself and the European. On certain issues, such as colonialism, the Africans and the Asians will probably make common cause. But I do not believe that there is any deep sense of 'racial brotherhood.' The Chinese, I suspect, is basically contemptuous of the African, and the African is fundamentally distrustful of the Chinese."

NIELSEN: "Could you compare British and

French economic aid in the same way you have Russian and Chinese?"

MR. X.: "I know very little about French assistance, since my country hasn't received any. It is clearly rather generous as far as the former French colonies are concerned, though apparently the French exact a considerable political price for the economic help they give.

"I do, however, have first-hand knowledge about the British and I think that what the British have done has been very good indeed. They have a practical sense of what is needed in Africa. They are careful in undertaking commitments, but once they do they can be relied upon to fulfill them. Also, I find the British rather satisfactory to do business with. They are not easy to make friends with, but after all these years they know us and we know them and we can usually come to terms.

"We have had great political differences with the British, as you know. But personally I have to say that the British have generally been very decent, and British help, both private investment and economic assistance, remains our single best hope in this country."

NIELSEN: "Would you give me your frank opinion about U.S. foreign aid to Africa?"

MR. X.: "You know, we Africans are still in the process of getting acquainted with you Americans. Up to a few years ago we had practically never seen an American except as an occasional big-game hunter or tourist. But after only brief acquaintance I have to say that you Americans are a puzzling lot. Your aid people here are terribly hard-working, terribly thorough and conscientious, terribly scientific. But I think also terribly bureaucratic.

"You make us produce more paper—plans, proposals, memoranda, analyses—than anybody else. Then in the end it seems that everything has to go to Washington for a decision. Many, many months go by before any project is approved, and when help does come it is usually disappointingly small.

"When a country is as hard-pressed as we are and when it has extremely few qualified people to work with, all of this is naturally very frustrating from our point of view."

NIELSEN: "What about the criticism that U.S. economic aid has too many political 'strings' attached?"

MR. X.: "I don't think there is much substance in that charge. The Russians, the Chinese, the French, the Germans are all more demanding, it seems to me, than the Americans.

"But this raises an interesting general question. Maybe you attach few political strings because you don't know what you want, politically. Frankly, I am quite confused as to your political objectives in giving economic aid to Africa. In some of your official statements it seems that you are trying to keep

Communism out of Africa. At other times it seems that you are trying to encourage what you call 'moderate' governments in Africa. But at other times you say you intend to give most of your help to those countries that have shown the best record of economic progress, regardless of their political coloration.

"These objectives are somewhat inconsistent, and certainly your actions seem to us to be very inconsistent. Again and again you have given your greatest help to countries that have abused the United States most—such as Ghana and Egypt. At the same time you have practically turned your back on countries that I consider to be genuinely moderate, like my own.

"We have seriously wondered at various times whether the only way to get an increase in American aid would be for us to criticize the United States vigorously in public and begin to make a show of sympathy for the Russians and the Chinese.

"May I make one further and rather indiscreet comment?"

NIELSEN: "Please do. I want to get as full an idea of your thinking as I can."

MR. X.: "I am particularly puzzled as to why a country as huge and powerful as yours seems to be so unsure of itself. The African gets the impression that the Americans want to be loved, want to be appreciated, want to be complimented. You seem to be particularly sensitive to criticism—and, on the other hand, particularly hungry for flattery and demonstrations of gratitude.

"We are appreciative—very appreciative—of the help your country has given us. But it is difficult for the recipient of help to prostrate himself at the feet of the donor. I wish more of your Congressmen and your private citizens back home could appreciate what I am trying to say."

NIELSEN: "Could we talk for a bit about trade, not aid, in relation to African economic development?"

MR. X.: "Excellent. Trade is more important to us and more crucial to development in Africa even than foreign aid."

NIELSEN: "What are the main problems as regards trade?"

MR. X.: "There are two that deeply concern me. First is the fact that my own country and most other African countries depend on one or two basic products that they have to sell abroad to earn their foreign exchange. In some cases we sell ore or minerals. In most cases we sell agricultural products—coffee, palm oil, cocoa and the like. This means that all of us are extremely dependent on the world market for our economic development.

"The second absolutely central point is that, in general, world market prices are going *down* for the kinds of products that we sell and going *up* for the kinds of products we buy. A statistic I came across the other day puts the matter dramatically and accurately. In 1958 Morocco had to export 200 tons of phosphate in order to pay for a single truck manufactured abroad. In 1963, however, it had to export 318 tons to pay for the same truck.

"The meaning of this is all too clear and ominous. We are caught in a tightening noose. To change the metaphor—we have to work harder and harder and run faster and faster just to stand still."

NIELSEN: "What can be done about it?"

MR. X.: "In practical fact I am afraid the situation will be extremely difficult to correct. There is little possibility, at least in the short run, for African countries to diversify their production and to get out from under dependence on the sale of one or two primary products in the world market. On the other hand, the big industrial countries show no willingness to join in measures to stabilize or improve the level of prices for the kinds of products which we in Africa have to sell.

"We had a huge meeting in Geneva under United Nations auspices in 1964 to discuss this problem. After a couple of days the delegates divided up into two opposing camps: those from countries that were trying to sell their products in the world market at declining prices and those from countries which sell their industrial products at increasing prices to the poorer countries. No progress was made.

"It will be hard enough to get the rich countries to increase their economic aid to us. But it will be five times as difficult to get them to do anything to improve world prices for the goods we have to sell. Your own country, along with the others, would much rather dole out economic aid than join in a scheme to put a floor under international coffee prices, for example. Yet from our point of view we would gladly give up all our foreign aid if we could just get a fairer price for what we have to sell overseas."

NIELSEN: "Apart from your problems of foreign aid and world trade, what would you say is the crucial obstacle to African economic progress in the future?"

MR. X.: "In one word, politics. If we can hold our internal situations together politically, we can make some headway. If we can't, I shudder to think of the consequences."

It can be somewhat disconcerting to listen to such a candid appraisal—but it can also be useful.

To obtain a fair and balanced answer to the question of how well Africa is doing in economic development I recently put a number of questions to a high official of an international economic agency. Neither African nor American, he is one of the world's wisest and most experienced men in this field. These were my questions and his answers:

NIELSEN: "Compared to other parts of the world, has Africa been receiving her fair share of economic aid from the major donor countries?"

MR. Y.: "On the whole, Africa has done better on a per-capita basis than most of the others. India, whose people are even poorer than those of Africa, has received about $1.50 per head per year of foreign aid in recent years. In comparison, the English-speaking African countries have been receiving about $3.00 per head per year and the French-speaking African countries still more than that per head per year."

NIELSEN: "Does that mean Africa has been receiving all she needs?"

MR. Y.: "Africa has been receiving all the aid she needs of certain kinds, such as capital loans. The African countries in general are so underdeveloped that they can 'absorb' only limited amounts of this kind of help until they get more trained people to develop and manage new projects.

"On the other hand, Africans could use vastly greater amounts of help in technical assistance and especially education and training."

NIELSEN: "How well has Africa done with the help she has received and through her own efforts?"

MR. Y.: "It is a little difficult to say because statistics in Africa are very uneven and all measurements are rather unreliable. But in general Africa is doing about as well as other underdeveloped regions. If our current estimates of population in Africa are accurate, this means that output is increasing a little faster than the number of people."

NIELSEN: "Which are the countries that you think are doing well and which are doing poorly?"

MR. Y.: "Speaking just of the countries of tropical and northern Africa, I would say that about fifteen are doing badly and have very little chance for real economic progress. About fifteen are doing moderately well and have fairly good chances for the future. Only four or five have really bright prospects.

"Among the brightest, I would say, are Ivory Coast, because of good resources and a very capable economic group in the government; Libya, because of the tremendous oil resources that have been discovered there; Nigeria, because of its resources and the general level of development of the population; and Zambia, where you have a combination of intelligent government and rich mineral resources, mainly copper.

"There are a number of other African countries where prospects in theory are good—such as the Congo, Liberia, Kenya, Ghana and Uganda—and where things may actually brighten considerably if they are able to work out some of their political kinks."

NIELSEN: "Which countries are at the bottom of the list?"

MR. Y.: "For the most part the areas that were formerly French colonies. A number are poor in resources—such as Niger and Chad. Some are just so tiny that they will never have a chance for economic survival unless they are somehow joined with larger areas. These include places like Togo, Upper Volta and Dahomey. So the picture is one of considerable variation, with bright spots and dark spots."

NIELSEN: "Looking to the future, what would you say the probabilities are?"

MR. Y.: "I am basically optimistic about the possibilities in Africa. The continent probably has a better chance to advance than most of the other underdeveloped regions. It starts from a somewhat better level of income than countries such as India, Pakistan or China. There is a better balance between population and land and other resources than in some of the other underdeveloped regions. Africa is more troubled with disease, but does not have the desperate nutritional problems found in some of the other regions.

"Compared to an area like Latin America, for example, Africa also has the benefit of a less rigid social structure and less ingrained hostility between the upper classes and the mass of the people."

NIELSEN: "As you look ahead to the coming few years, what will be the major obstacle to African economic progress?"

MR. Y.: "Politics and political disorders."

* * *

That was the same danger cited by my African friend. Let us then take a closer look at the political currents which are moving in the newly independent African nations—currents which may carry forward their hopes for economic progress or which may dash them on the rocks.

VI

The Rocky Road to Democracy

"WE ARE GOING to show the world what the black man can do when he works in freedom. . . .

"We are going to reexamine all the former laws and from them make new laws which will be noble and just. . . .

"We are going to put an end to the oppression of free thought, so that all citizens may enjoy fully the fundamental liberties provided for in the Declaration of the Rights of Man. . . ."

These were the hopeful words of the Premier of the Congo, Patrice Lumumba, in mid-1960. And these were the goals of the struggle for independence throughout Africa.

But in country after country, beginning almost immediately after independence, factional violence broke out; deadly quarrels raged among African leaders; and one by one the new states, almost without exception, turned away from democracy as we know it and toward the creation of one-party states —governments which in varying degrees restrict the rights of political opposition.

Cameroun: During 1962, the arrest and imprisonment of the principal opposition leaders in the eastern part of the country converted it, for all practical purposes, into a one-party state.

Central African Republic: In November, 1962 the cabinet officially dissolved several opposition parties and decreed that the country would henceforth be a one-party state.

Chad: Formation of new opposition parties was banned by presidential decree in 1962. A year later, opposition politicians were arrested and imprisoned.

The list could go on and on. In some of the new countries the opposition has been outlawed. In others it has joined the government—but under greater or lesser compulsion. In some it has been jailed. And in some the opposition chose—or was forced into—exile. In country after country the government has restricted the freedom of the press, has taken control of trade unions and youth organizations and in some instances has interfered with the independence of the judiciary. President Kwame

Nkrumah of Ghana, who earlier had said that he sought to establish his party "as the democratic instrument of the people's will and aspirations," himself overruled his own supreme court in 1965, ordering the retrial of five of his chief opponents. Although these men had originally been acquitted, the court compliantly sentenced them to death, though Nkrumah later commuted the sentence.

The dramatic and almost total collapse of experiments with Western-style democracy in Africa forces us to ask whether our kind of democracy can really be transplanted to such different societies. Can democracy exist in the emergent countries, where economic improvement and internal stability are so urgently necessary?

For Americans such questions are fundamental. The idea of democracy, however vaguely defined, has come to be an article of faith in the United States. We tend to think of it as an absolute virtue, necessary to any kind of progress. In this century we claim to have fought one world war to make the world safe for it and a second to resist governments that were evil opposites of it. In the countries of our recently conquered enemies, Germany and Japan, we went to great lengths to root out totalitarian ideas and replace them with democratic concepts.

When colonialism ended in Africa we, along with many others, experienced a great wave of optimism and sympathy for the new states. But the subsequent collapse of democratic forms caused an exaggerated swing of feeling in the opposite direction—pessimism replaced hope, dismay and disrespect replaced admiration. To explain what has gone wrong some non-Africans have smugly concluded that the black African is barbarous, uncivilized and simply incapable of democratic citizenship. Their scorn reminds me of a statement made by the American Negro comedian Dick Gregory: "You gotta say this for the white race—its self-confidence knows no bounds. Who else could go to a small island in the South Pacific where there is no poverty, no crime, no unemployment, no war and no worry—and call it a 'primitive society'?"

The devotion of some Africans to civilized life is rooted in history. One Arab traveler, Ibn Batuta, wrote of the Mali empire in 1352 that its Negroes ". . . are seldom unjust, and have a greater horror of injustice than other people. Their sultan shows no mercy to anyone who is guilty of the least act of it. There is complete security in their country. Neither traveler nor inhabitant in it has anything to fear from robbers or men of violence. . . ."

Before we dismiss the Africans as "primitives" who are unready for self-government we might also consider the record of Europeans on the Dark Continent and the examples they have set in the recent past and still offer today.

Item: During the seven-year war in Algeria, which ended in 1962, the French army developed highly refined methods of torture such as the so-called "electric bathtub" which reduced its victims to mindlessness. Certain tribal customs of warfare are more colorful perhaps than those of the more industrialized countries, but the unhappy fact is that —whether African or non-African—all humanity seems equally capable of barbarous inhumanity on occasion.

Item: The most undemocratic states on the African continent are still those controlled by whites, not by Africans. Rhodesia, one of these areas, is among the more gentle in its repression of the blacks; there, nevertheless, some 2,000 African nationalist leaders are being kept in prison or detention to prevent them from organizing and leading popular protest movements. Mozambique and Angola, under the Portuguese, suppress the political rights of virtually all the population and by the most brutal methods. It is estimated that from 50,000 to 135,000 Africans were machinegunned, beaten or burned to death in 1961 by the Portuguese in reprisal against a political uprising in Angola.

And the conditions of the African worker in the Portuguese areas has been described by a former high official of the Portuguese government, Captain Henrique Galvão, in these words: "In some ways the situation is worse than simple slavery. Under slavery, after all, the native is bought as an animal: his owner prefers him to remain as fit as a horse or an ox. Yet here the native is not bought—he is hired from the State, although he is called a free man. And his employer cares little if he sickens or dies once he is working because when he sickens or dies his employer will simply ask for another."

Item: In South Africa the undemocratic idea has been carried to its ultimate point: not only have the political and economic rights and personal dignity of the African been destroyed, but it has been made illegal for him to protest, *even by peaceable means,* the deprivation of liberty to which he has been subjected.

To explain away the decline of democracy in Africa by saying that the black man is essentially a barbarian and a child is therefore unconvincing. It is also unconvincing to say that freedom is failing because Africa's current leaders are cynical, power-hungry politicians without devotion to democratic ideals.

There are some African heads of state who could be called power-hungry politicians—and even a couple who could probably be called scoundrels. On the other hand, there are outstanding leaders whose devotion to democracy is deep and strong. I remember once talking with Nnamdi Azikiwe, President of the Republic of Nigeria, in his office in Lagos. He is a tall impressive man, doubly impressive in the flowing white robe he wears. He strode up and down his paneled office as he described his philosophy of government: "To me, democracy, like music, is one of the universal languages of mankind. I am convinced that it is the wave of the future—particularly because of its appeal to young people. All over the world, and here in Africa too, the young people have really fallen in love with democracy. But I always say to them that it is not enough just to believe in it, you must work for it. What we need are not only disciples of democracy but apostles of democracy."

On the whole, the leaders of the new nations of Africa—measured by their idealism, intellect and innate ability—are an extraordinary group of men. Many have come from simple families and are self-educated. Many have known at first hand the poverty and backward conditions of the countryside; many spent years in prison under colonial governors.

Nor is it surprising that many of them feel a fundamental sympathy for democratic and Christian concepts. Most received their primary and secondary education in schools supported by missionaries. Others received their early training under headmasters formed in the Western tradition. Those who received higher education before assuming their present positions of leadership did so almost without exception at European or American universities. Their understanding of democratic political values is therefore no mere gloss or pose; some of these men have been steeped in it since their childhood. That leaders of this background and character have nevertheless in many cases now openly advocated one-party government is perhaps the most distressing fact of all for Americans, a fact which forces us to think deeply about the causes.

What happened? We cannot say that these leaders were in no way infected by the age-old tendency of men, once in power, to punish their political enemies and to seek to perpetuate their control. But we should also look to some of the real and immediate problems they faced. These include the problems of national unity, of internal factional warfare and of violent political opposition.

"Unity"—in the sense of attaching the loyalty of individual citizens to new symbols of nationhood— is not easily achieved in Africa. In Tanganyika, for example, after independence a national anthem had to be written, a flag had to be invented and there was not even a word in the local language, Swahili, for saying "Tanganyikan." That too had to be manufactured. Three years later, when Tanganyika merged with its island neighbor Zanzibar, new symbols of loyalty had to be created for the new nation of Tanzania.

Before they achieved independence the peoples of the new African nations were united by their common feeling against the foreigner. But afterward

that glue came unstuck. Old tribal and ethnic antag-
onisms broke out in many areas almost simultaneously with the beginning of national political activity. In Burundi and Rwanda there have been
repeated conflicts between the seven-foot-tall Watusis
and the majority Bahutu tribe. In Zanzibar there
were bloody riots between Arabs and Africans in
the first election in 1961 and again in 1964. In the
Sudan there has been harsh repression of the southern African minority by the northern Arab majority.
Hostility between the three major tribes in Nigeria
has almost torn that country apart. Throughout the
newly independent areas of Africa parallel cases
could be cited.

In Africa national unity has also been threatened
repeatedly by actual attempts at secession and open
rebellion, often from border areas far from the capital where the central government could not exercise
effective control. The United States had some 70
years to organize itself and put down roots before it
had to cope with such problems. Some new African
nations—Uganda, Mali, Chad, Upper Volta, the
Congo and others—sometimes did not have 70 days.

Decades before it achieved independence the
United States had begun to acquire experience in
the settling of internal political differences by compromise and peaceful agreement. Few of the new
African states had that advantage; for most of them
independence came suddenly without a prior period

of preparation. Consequently, those who disagree
with their own new government have often tended
to use the political methods learned during the process of revolution against colonialism. Even a partial
list of the violent actions of political opposition in
recent years in Africa is sobering.

Sylvanus Olympio, the President of Togo, Patrice
Lumumba in the Congo, and others have been killed.
Other assassination attempts have been reported in
Ivory Coast, Liberia, Chad and Niger. President
Nkrumah of Ghana in his first eight years in office
survived two bombs, a hand grenade and point-
blank rifle shots.

Several efforts to take over governments by force
have already been successful—in the Sudan in
1958; in Togo, the former French Congo and Dahomey in 1963; and in Zanzibar in 1964. Other
coups have been attempted but for one reason or
another have failed in, among others, Ethiopia in
1960; Senegal in 1962; the Ivory Coast, Chad and
Niger in 1963; and Gabon, Tanganyika, Uganda
and Kenya in 1964. There have also been arrests,
charges of plots and treason trials in Nigeria,
Guinea, Ivory Coast and elsewhere.

Keeping in mind such a catalogue of difficulties, it
should not be surprising to find that many African
leaders have felt that some restraint—by force if
necessary—should be imposed on the exuberance of
political strife. In some cases they may have pro-

voked violent opposition by their own misconduct and in some instances may have "invented" coups or assassination attempts in order to dispose of their political enemies. Nevertheless, the problem of reckless, irresponsible opposition in many of the new countries has represented a genuine threat to their continued existence and to orderly if not representative government.

Indifference to the needs of a new nation can be quite as threatening as violent opposition. In some countries the people outside the cities have resisted change of any kind. Many Africans claim that the one-party state offers important advantages in overcoming this sluggishness and resistance. By linking women's organizations, youth movements, labor unions and all other groups into a single national movement they have hoped to generate a dynamic spirit which could move their countries forward.

Related to this is the feeling on the part of some leaders that a one-party state can impose necessary discipline on the population and prevent the dissipation of national energies in uncoordinated efforts and in fruitless squabbling. Once in power and faced with serious difficulty in getting their development programs moving, a number of African leaders have come to place increasing emphasis on the need for such discipline.

Dr. H. Kamuzu Banda of Malawi, once one of the most fiery spokesmen for freedom, has now become a sturdy advocate of practicality, even of conservatism, in managing the affairs of his new country. I remember his telling me in his house in Blantyre after he had become President:

"I was once a very bad boy in the eyes of the British—but I knew it was only by being a bad boy that I could get what I wanted, namely, independence for Malawi. Now that that has been achieved, I am prepared to behave myself. Moreover, I assure you that I intend to see that others in Malawi behave themselves too. The time has come for working together. There is no place, now that we are free, for anyone who would seek to tear down what we have so painfully been able to build up."

Another indication of the same tendency to stress discipline and responsibility occurred recently when the students of Upper Volta were holding a congress in the national capital, Ouagadougou, during which many militant and highly critical speeches were made about the government. On the last day, the President of the country, Maurice Yameogo, unexpectedly arrived and addressed them: "During the whole of this conference you have behaved like spoiled children," he said. "I was perfectly aware what was said every day upon this platform, but I have held back and allowed this congress to go on to its end to prove democracy is not an empty word in Upper Volta and to learn better what is biting you. I therefore have this to say to you: you have amused yourselves nicely. You have spat well on everybody. But now the fun and games are over, for your brothers of the Volta labor daily to pay for your studies and not to launch you on a criminal enterprise of demolition."

Thus the leaders of the new Africa are gropingly trying to deal with the deep problems they face: the need for modernization versus the fact of backwardness, the need for unity versus the fact of political and social division, and, in many cases, the desire for democracy versus the need for rapid development and civil order. Their dilemma is reflected even in the criticism of the outside world, which in one breath deplores disorder and irresponsibility and in the next condemns the imposition of restraints.

Yet, however well-meaning their efforts may be, the fact remains that many of the new leaders have tampered with the political rights and principles that lie at the very heart of freedom and democratic government—including the rights of free speech and assembly, freedom of the press, the independence of the judiciary and the rule of law.

Some scholars have sought to justify these excesses and aberrations. They point out that although the one-party states of Africa are not liberal in their practices they are by no means totalitarian. The citizens do not live in terror of a secret police, and where severe measures of repression have been taken they were "required" by the excesses of destructive opposition elements. They point out also that within the single-party systems there is often active discussion and free debate of issues. Party membership is typically unrestricted and open to anyone. Also, in accordance with African tradition, the practice is commonly followed of taking action only after a wide degree of consensus has been achieved. In brief, those inclined to take an uncritical view of political trends in Africa emphasize that invasions of democratic rights have been limited and necessary, that there is more democratic participation in their processes than at first appears, and that the one-party state in many ways is in accord with African tribal traditions of political debate within a single structure of authority.

But it should also be pointed out that some Africans vigorously disagree with all efforts to excuse the political trends under way. Chief Awolowo of Nigeria, a prominent political leader in the early struggles for independence of that country, has now been imprisoned after what he and his friends regard as a "political trial" at the hands of the present government. He rejects totally the idea that "African democracy" should be a compromise version of democracy elsewhere.

"There is a new-fangled theory now being propounded with erudition and gusto in the countries of the so-called Western democracies," he has written.

"The proponents of this theory hold the view that it is inappropriate and hardly fair to expect a newly emergent African nation to practice democracy as it is known and practiced in the countries of Western Europe and the United States of America. Every mortal blow that is struck by an independent African nation at the vitals of democracy is rationalized by these theorists as the African's peculiar method of adapting democratic usages to his barbaric and primitive environment. The denial of fundamental human rights, the destruction of the rule of law and the suppression of opposition have been brilliantly and felicitously rationalized. The outrageous declaration by an African leader that a one-party system is in accord with the democratic way of life has been ably defended by these spokesmen of the Western democracies."

Whether what has happened and is happening to democracy in Africa is justified or not by urgent needs for stability and development is clearly a matter of tangled and passionate debate. But, given the present trends, what will happen next? Will time prove that independence was the prelude to freedom —or to the mere replacement of foreign political domination by a new crop of local dictators?

First, it seems clear that, whether democratic or not, one-party states and the personalization of political power in most of Africa will continue for a long time to come.

Second, it is the Africans themselves, now that they are independent, who will have to develop their own political patterns and set their own priorities as between democracy and discipline. It is likely that the forms that will develop will be at variance with many familiar Western political practices. And it is unlikely that, in the foreseeable future, democratic principles will be given priority over practical needs for unity, stability and development. In a few cases, such as Sierra Leone and perhaps Nigeria, recognizable democratic standards will be maintained, but in most places they will not.

Democracy has been a great human dream over the centuries. But it has infrequently been practiced and it has repeatedly succumbed to other pressures, ideas and requirements. If the prospects for democracy in the Western sense are not bright in the period ahead in Africa, that may be displeasing and difficult for many Americans to accept. But, given the present state of the world, it should not be astonishing. Nor should it be overwhelmingly discouraging; the desire for political freedom in Africa is not dead, and in time it may yet find its means of full expression.

VII

The Congo—Cockpit of the Continent

IN EARLY 1962, during one of the Congo's crises, I stayed for a few days with Edmund A. Gullion, who was then the American Ambassador in Leopoldville. The Embassy residence is on the banks of the Congo River, which reaches 2,000 miles into the heart of that vast country. The great river was in flood and where it flowed past the Ambassador's home it was several miles wide.

As he and I looked across the moving waters we saw enormous clumps of hyacinths, some of them several acres in area, going downstream. They passed like colorful floats in a pageant and their perfume filled the air of the whole city.

The Ambassador told me that a few years earlier some missionary families upcountry had brought

hyacinth plants over from the United States to adorn
their gardens. The hyacinth and the Congo climate
made a natural marriage. Soon the hyacinths had
spread like weeds throughout the interior, eventually choking many of the smaller tributary streams.
The floods had ripped the flowers from their roots
and were taking them down by the millions to the
ocean.

Not every contact between the Congo and the
white outsider has produced such picturesque consequences. From the very beginning, in fact, with the
white man has usually come trouble for the Congo.

Portuguese explorers were the first to come to the
area now known as the Congo. After them came the
missionaries, sent by the King in Lisbon to Christianize the natives. One young prince of the great
Congo kingdom, Afonso, studied for ten years under Portuguese priests, becoming fluent in their language, knowledgeable in European history and a
devoted Christian. When he became king, he tried
his best to bring the benefits of European civilization to his people.

But both the missionaries and the Portuguese soldiers soon forgot their Christianizing purpose and
became increasingly involved with the richly profitable traffic in slaves. As the white man ravaged his
people, Afonso sent pitiful pleas to Lisbon and to
Rome, which were ignored. In the end he died a
frustrated and disillusioned monarch; the bright

promise of Christianity had become but a memory, and his once great tribe had shriveled to a few miserable villages lost in the wilderness.

The modern Belgians did somewhat better. Their record as a colonial power from 1908 until 1960, when the Congo became independent, is a curious tale of both kindness and greed. That story—and the first years following the birth of the new African nation—deserves retelling in some detail not only because of its headline drama but because it is a classic case rich in lessons and warnings for the future of all Africa.

The Congo, strategically located in the heart of Africa and as large as Western Europe, is one of the richest areas in the world in minerals and material resources. After decades of Belgian rule the Congo became independent in 1960, and its troubles ever since have been an object of concern throughout the world. The United Nations peacekeeping operation in the Congo was the most concentrated and expensive ever undertaken by the world organization, costing $400 million, of which the U.S. contributions were more than 40 per cent. Still today the country is racked with the struggle of finding its own formula for stability. Understanding the Congo can do much to deepen our grasp of the problems of Africa, present and future.

The Belgians governed the colony by dividing it into three spheres: business would be responsible

for economic development; the churches, primarily
Roman Catholic, would be responsible for education; and the state—that is, Belgium—would be responsible for roads, transport, public services and
the maintenance of order. The results of the system,
in economic terms, were remarkable. Industry and
agriculture prospered, and by 1959 the living standards of the Congolese were probably higher than
those of any other black people in Africa. The government maintained order through the tightly disciplined *Force Publique,* manned by Africans and
officered by Belgians. Extensive social and welfare
services were provided, and a large-scale housing
program virtually eliminated slums in the cities. Belgian achievement in education in the Congo were
unparalleled: by the late nineteen-fifties nearly 50
per cent of the Congolese were literate, an extremely high figure for Africa. But Belgium cut off
higher education to all but a few Congolese for fear
of opening the door to dissatisfaction and political
agitation. This educational philosophy contains a
clue to why, in the end, Belgium's methods in the
Congo failed. As early as 1953 an American of wide
experience in foreign affairs, Chester Bowles, saw the
dangers in Belgium's policy. He pointed out that it
would not prevent dissatisfaction and that on the inevitable day of independence there would be too
few qualified Congolese to run the country.

Despite the care taken by Belgium to insulate the

Congo from outside political contact, and despite the material well-being of the population, the demand for independence gradually began to spread throughout the country, especially after World War II. Sporadic signs of discontent were followed by organized protest. Social and discussion groups and student clubs began to form. These were set up on a local or tribal basis because national African organizations were forbidden. In these clubs many leaders later to become prominent in the Congo received their first training.

One was a young man named Joseph Kasavubu, later to become President of the new Congo Republic. While still a clerk in the colonial government he led a demand for "equal pay for equal work for Africans." And from the beginning he was a strong spokesman for regional autonomy, especially for the Bakongo area from which he came.

Another was Patrice Lumumba, whose political base was the northern city of Stanleyville. He had only a primary-school education and became a postal clerk. One African expert, Colin Legum, once described him as "a tall rake of a man, with a tiny, narrow head and a chinful of beard. . . . His manner is lively and vital; his smile is light and quick and frequent. . . . His tongue is silver; he talks rapidly and ceaselessly. But his easy, pleasant manner is deceptive; Lumumba is earnest and tough and capable, if the need should arise, of being ruthless."

He became strongly anti-Belgian, but as late as 1957, while being held by the Belgians in jail, Lumumba wrote: "We must get it into our heads that in the Congo, without the Blacks, the Whites are of no value, and without the Whites, the Blacks have no value either. This economic interdependence makes union necessary for us. Our dearest wish—perhaps some may find it Utopian—is to found in the Congo a Nation in which differences in race and religion will melt away, a homogeneous society composed of Belgians and Congolese, who with a single impulse will link their hearts to the destinies of the country. . . ."

In the mid-nineteen-fifties, as political discontent increased, the Belgians began cautiously to permit limited African participation in local government. Then an eminent Belgian professor, Dr. Van Bilsen, created a storm of controversy in 1955 by mentioning the forbidden word "independence" and suggesting Congolese self-government within 30 years.

In 1956 a small African newspaper in Leopoldville, *Conscience Africaine,* published a manifesto which echoed Van Bilsen's proposal. The Belgian authorities regarded the manifesto as nonsense and made no reply. They believed that Belgian rule would last another hundred years. But the mood of the Congolese population was reflected in the fact that news of the manifesto swept through the African cities and deep into the bush country. Africans who couldn't read pasted copies on their walls; and the manifesto sold at football games like hot cakes.

By 1957 the Belgian government began to institute reforms: more freedom of speech and press for the Africans; outlawing of racial discrimination; widened African participation in governmental affairs. But public discontent grew even faster and disorders developed in various parts of the country.

By January, 1959, the Belgian government proposed a five-year plan for independence. One year later, at a round-table conference in Brussels with Congolese leaders, Belgium accepted a demand for independence within six months, or June 30, 1960. In the absence of any plan or timetable for independence the Belgians had in less than four years shifted from almost total resistance to demands for independence to virtually total surrender. Thus a bizarre example of confused colonialism came to its end.

When the Congo got its independence it was not a nation in any real sense. The loyalties of the people were to tribe and locality. The population was politically inexperienced. In the rush toward independence the process by which tribal loyalties might have been transferred to the nation—such as by a succession of national elections with African participation—was skipped over entirely.

At that crucial moment the lack of trained leadership became a glaring danger. The average education of the Africans who participated in the round-table meeting at Brussels was less than high-school level. There were 12 Congolese university graduates in the entire country at the time of independence, and in the first cabinet under Premier Lumumba there was only one man with a university degree.

One of the most unfortunate consequences of the planless stampede to independence was the fear and bitterness engendered between Belgians and Congolese. As the day of the independence celebration approached there were increasing acts of violence against whites in many parts of the country. Thus what should have been a day of national rejoicing was instead a time of fear and hostility. Terrible prophecies circulated—that white estates were to be plundered, white women raped and white men massacred. Europeans were in such a state of psychological tension that general panic was feared at the first incident.

Lumumba, the onetime friend of Belgium, made a harsh speech at the flag-raising celebration in the presence of the Belgian king: "Our lot was 80 years of colonial rule; our wounds are still too fresh and painful to be driven from our memory. . . . We have known ironies, insults, blows which we had to endure, morning, noon and night, because we were 'Negroes.' . . . Today we are no longer your Makal [monkeys]."

That independence under the circumstances

would lead directly to chaos was sensed by many. Some Belgians in the Congo expressed their feelings in caustic criticism of their own government. One wrote: "The truth is that the Belgian government, whatever may be its reasons, wants to rid itself of the Congo. That could perhaps be justified. But what is criminal on its part is its hypocritical deliverance of the Congo into disorder, anarchy, and impoverishment, and to do it only to be able to wash its hands, like Pontius Pilate, of the future of the Congo. . . ."

In the two weeks following independence the worst fears were confirmed. All the sins and errors of the Belgians and all the faults and foolishness of the Congolese combined to produce total disaster. As a classic case of chaos in a new country, consider the following calendar:

July 1—Independence.

July 4—Minor tribal disorders reported in Leopoldville and elsewhere.

July 5—Increased tribal disorders and first rumors of a revolt on the part of the Force Publique.

July 6—Open revolt of the Force Publique, demanding higher pay, promotions and the removal of Belgian officers.

July 8—Panic among the Europeans, with thousands fleeing Leopoldville.

July 10—Belgian forces intervene in Leopoldville to restore order, and paratroopers are dropped in various parts of the Congo.

July 11—Moise Tshombe declares secession of Katanga Province from the Congo and accuses the central government of trying to establish a "ruinous and Communist state."

July 12—Congo Vice-Premier Gizenga requests direct U.S. military assistance; President Eisenhower refuses and refers Congo leaders to the U.N. President Kasavubu then cables the United Nations requesting the "urgent dispatch" of United Nations military assistance and denouncing the dispatch of Belgian troops to the Congo as "an act of aggression."

July 13—Lumumba and Kasavubu order all Belgian troops to return to their camps—an order which is ignored—and cable the United Nations that if a U.N. military force is not sent to the Congo without delay they will appeal to the Communist countries for help.

July 14—The United Nations Security Council authorizes the Secretary General, Dag Hammarskjold, to provide military assistance to the Congo in addition to technical aid.

July 15—The first United Nations troops arrive in Leopoldville.

In those two weeks the new country had been hit by quadruple disaster: the breakdown of civil order, army revolt, secession and external military intervention.

Young Patrice Lumumba, who earlier had shown such powers of leadership and a clear understanding of the need to weld the Congo into a single nation, proved unable in his inexperience to cope with the multiplying problems. His behavior became erratic. He gave orders which he promptly countermanded; he announced policies which in the next breath he reversed. Allegations, charges, appeals, declarations of all kinds poured from his mouth and pen during frantic weeks when he lived almost without sleep, surviving on drink and hemp smoking.

After the declaration of secession by Moise Tshombe in Katanga, Lumumba wanted the United Nations troops to take the copper-rich province by force. At that stage the United Nations was not yet ready to use its troops for such a purpose, and Lumumba, from the moment he discovered he could not use its forces as he wished, lost faith in the United Nations. Even with the highest representatives of the organization his manner became rude and insulting, especially toward Dr. Ralph Bunche and Mr. Dag Hammarskjold.

The Katanga secession was followed by indications of secession by other provinces. Watching the country beginning to disintegrate, Lumumba became desperate. Without the knowledge of his colleagues in the government he called for Soviet planes and tanks to come to his aid—and this was his undoing. In early September President Kasavubu ousted Lumumba as Premier and called on the United Nations to take over all responsibility for law and order. Lumumba refused to accept his removal, and a struggle with Kasavubu ensued. To end the confusion the Congolese armed forces under General Joseph Mobutu seized power in mid-September. Mobutu promptly ordered all Communist representatives out of the country, closed the Parliament and subsequently arrested Lumumba.

In the next two and a half years the United Nations, in addition to its peacekeeping operations, tried through technical and economic assistance to bring order out of chaos. Its non-military achievements during that period have largely been overlooked. The United Nations' 1,300 doctors, teachers and technicians filled a crucial need, especially in the first months after the wholesale withdrawal of panic-stricken Belgian administrators. The United Nations staff carried on emergency distribution of food, cared for refugees and even helped draft a new constitution.

During this period two personal tragedies occurred. In February, 1961, Lumumba tried to escape from Mobutu's control. He was caught and killed while crossing a part of rural Katanga—and a heavy suspicion has hung since over Tshombe. In September, 1961, U.N. Secretary General Hammarskjold en route to negotiations with Tshombe, perished in a mysterious air crash.

The United Nations had had a most difficult time agreeing on a policy of strong military action to deal with the problem of Katanga, and Hammarskjold's death immobilized the United Nations for months while the great powers decided on his successor.

Finally in January, 1963, and as a result of United Nations military action coupled with complex diplomatic efforts, the Katanga secession collapsed. The Congo again became a single political entity and for the first time since 1960 the country's problems disappeared from the headlines of the world's press. Tshombe left the country to live in Europe, his political career apparently at an end.

Once again the slow task of binding up the country's wounds and organizing its affairs began. But the violence and passion in the Congo's early years of independence were hard to forget. The Belgians felt humiliated by the vilification directed at them. The Soviet Union was resentful of the United Nations, which it believed had been used as an instrument of "Western imperialism." In the United States, opinion was divided. Tshombe had been portrayed as an anti-Communist stalwart, and some Americans felt our policy had been wrong in helping to depose him. Other critics objected in principle to the use of military force by the United Nations to accomplish its "peacekeeping objective." And throughout many parts of the U.S. there was disquiet because for the first time a major commitment of

American prestige and resources had been made in the remoteness of tropical Africa.

Within the Congo there was malaise and confusion. The population was disillusioned with the first fruits of independence. There was resentment against the Belgians and growing resentment between various areas and elements of the country. Suspicion of the United Nations and bitterness over the circumstances of Lumumba's death were widespread.

All these fears, frustrations and hard feelings, temporarily obscured by the reunification of the country, were to erupt again.

The role of the United Nations in the Congo is most difficult—and most important—to understand. The United Nations had been called into the Congo in desperation when the situation was already in flames. As the eminent British diplomat Lord Caradon has said, "The United Nations is handed problems only after the countries directly involved have completely mucked them up. And then as soon as the U.N. takes over, everybody, and especially the Great Powers, do all they can to criticize, obstruct, and interfere with the U.N.'s work."

There is no doubt that the United Nations effort in the Congo was successful in accomplishing most of its objectives: it restored civil order and public services; it prevented a major cold-war confrontation in the heart of Africa; and it preserved the territorial unity of the country. On the other hand, the efforts of the United Nations to restrain the Congolese army and to provide a competent corps of Congolese administrators to take over were less successful, largely because of the shortness of time and because United Nations member countries were unwilling to provide clear directives and sufficient funds for economic aid and training.

As soon as the Katanga secession was quelled the impulse of the member countries was to withdraw U.N. forces and personnel. Thus, paradoxically, having taken on a thankless and nearly hopeless task and having done it creditably, the U.N. was first handcuffed and then withdrawn. The last of the United Nations troops left the Congo in June, 1964, and only enough funds to maintain a skeleton corps of civilian technicians in the country could be raised.

Perhaps the clearest proof of United Nations usefulness is the fact that promptly after its withdrawal the Congo once again fell into violent disorder. And in an ironic turn of events the enigmatic Tshombe was called upon to become premier, replacing the competent but colorless Cyrille Adoula, who had held the country together through skillful compromise during three arduous years.

The New York Times editorially summarized the situation: "When the Belgians left on July 1, 1960, the Congo, like Humpty Dumpty, fell off and all the

U.N.'s forces and all the U.N.'s men could not put it together again. The U.N. made a valiant effort, which for a while seemed to be succeeding. . . . Tshombe was forced out of Katanga Province and Leopoldville nominally became the core of a centralized government. Yet when the U.N. forces had to quit just four years after they had begun, the Congo was falling apart again. Moise Tshombe, returning as Premier, is now in his turn facing a secessionist move."

This secession was in the form of a spreading rebellion centered in the northern and eastern parts of the country, led by former followers of Patrice Lumumba and allegedly assisted with supplies of arms and money by the Communist states, particularly China. By fall of 1964 the rebels were in control of large portions of the northeastern Congo.

Tshombe's methods of dealing with the civil war confronting him showed again why he is one of the most important and controversial figures in Africa. He first appealed to the African states for military help and was refused. He then promptly recruited a corps of white "mercenaries" from South Africa, Rhodesia and elsewhere. He obtained aircraft from the United States, which he manned with anti-Castro Cuban pilots.

For many Africans these actions, confirmed the suspicion that Tshombe was a "stooge" for white colonial and financial interests, that he was contemptuous of Africa and Africans and that he was a "traitor" to African nationalism and independence.

But his self-confidence, his energy, his political agility and his abundant willingness to seek realistic solutions to urgent problems were also characteristic. Moreover, his military methods achieved some success. In a matter of weeks his mercenary-led troops drove the rebels back to a few small pockets of territory, the center of which was the northern city of Stanleyville. There, in late November, occurred an explosive and politically destructive event.

The situation was this: Tshombe's troops were advancing on Stanleyville, the rebel capital. The rebel leaders, increasingly desperate, appealed to the principal association of independent African states, the Organization of African Unity (O.A.U.), for help and mediation. At the same time these rebel leaders seized the hundreds of whites in the area as hostages, threatening to burn them in gasoline if the Western powers, especially Belgium and the United States, did not persuade Tshombe to halt the advance of his forces.

The Western countries in the preceding weeks had become increasingly aware of isolated acts of violence directed against European missionaries and nuns in rebel-held territories. The Belgian government, whose nationals accounted for the larger part of the white community in the Stanleyville area, carried on intensive negotiations with the rebel regime, urging that it not violate the Geneva Conventions intended to protect civilians in areas of conflict and specifically prohibiting the taking of hostages. The United States meanwhile had become aroused by the case of Dr. Paul E. Carlson, an American missionary doctor condemned to death by the rebels on charges of spying. The rebels rejected all appeals— and the Belgian and American governments finally decided in November to act to protect their citizens. The events which followed are a vivid example of how the same set of facts can be viewed and interpreted in totally different ways, depending on the national eyeglasses through which they are seen.

As the United States and Belgium saw the matter, what was done was a proper and necessary humanitarian action. The danger was imminent and last-minute negotiations had collapsed. At the invitation of the Congolese government in Leopoldville, Belgian paratroops were flown to Stanleyville in American planes at dawn on November 24. Their mission was to rescue hostages. During the one-day operation nearly 1,700 persons were freed. Approximately 80 hostages, including Dr. Carlson, were killed by the rebels. Within three days Belgian troops were withdrawn.

In the Western view the rescue action was taken only after every other avenue to secure the safety of innocent people had been closed by rebel intransigence. The sole purpose of the action, according to the United States, was to accomplish its humanitarian task quickly and withdraw.

But from the point of view of a number of African states the whole affair appeared in a quite different light. To them the Stanleyville group were not rebels but true African nationalists. The purpose of the Belgian-American paratroop operation was not humanitarian but military—to help the traitorous Tshombe's white mercenaries capture the nationalist capital. Africans pointed out that the airdrop closely coincided with the arrival in Stanleyville of Tshombe's troops, who in the days following captured many towns in the area and massacred hundreds of rebel partisans and Congolese civilians.

The idea that Tshombe had "authorized" the airdrop was rejected as a cynical hoax; in the African view, Tshombe the puppet had been forced to accept foreign military intervention and to surrender the sovereignty of the Congo. Africans resented also the apparent slight to their O.A.U., which, under a committee headed by Kenya's Jomo Kenyatta, was attempting to work out a negotiated solution to the differences between Tshombe and the Stanleyville leaders at the very moment the airdrop was conducted.

In the ensuing days resentments and emotions exploded, mobs were incited to attack U.S. Embassies, charges and countercharges crackled in the press and assemblies of the world. *Time* Magazine lost control of itself, saying that the murder of Dr. Carlson proved that ". . . Black African civilization— with its elaborate trappings of half a hundred sovereignties, governments and U.N. delegations—is largely a pretense. . . ," and added: "When this happened, the sane part of the world could only wonder whether Black Africa can be taken seriously at all, or whether, for the foreseeable future, it is beyond the reach of reason."

African feelings and journalistic expression were equally fervent. *The Nationalist,* a newspaper published in Tanzania, said the American attitude toward Africa "approximates increasingly to the sort of attitude represented by those who believe in racial superiority, even if it is cloaked by a sort of supercilious paternalism. Do we have to go to Mississippi or the Southern States of America to see well-trained dogs unleashed on non-whites to convince ourselves who the savages are?" In frustration and hate a representative of Mali said at the United Nations: "We do not believe that the black minority in the United States of America enjoys as many rights in American society as the inhabitants of Tibet enjoy in the People's Republic of China."

Within a few days politicians, diplomats, journalists and others began to regain a degree of balance and perspective. On the American side it was still felt that the actions taken had been justified and necessary—but a new awareness of African sensibilities was created.

On the African side some regimes, including the government of Nigeria, spoke out understandingly about the humanitarian aspects of the airdrop. They also criticized the tendency of certain African states to interfere in the affairs of others and to attack leaders with whom they disagreed.

The aftermath of the accusations, fears and frustrations provoked by the Stanleyville incident would not soon be forgotten and their ghosts may yet rise to haunt the troubled Congo.

But out of the confusion, the agony and the turmoil a few lessons have become clear:

Sudden, unplanned independence can be a tragedy for the people of a former colony and a danger to the whole world. This lesson underscores the need for urgent efforts to train leaders and prepare the African countries south of the Congo for independence. Otherwise a series of Congo-like disorders may occur.

The United Nations has proved its value as an instrument for preventing local disorders from becoming major dangers to world peace. The growing division of the U.N., which paralyzed its General Assembly in 1965, is therefore an ominous development. If the United Nations is not available to step into the breach in future Congos, the danger to world peace will be grave.

The United States must continue patiently and sometimes expensively to participate fully in international actions in key areas such as the Congo. We cannot become involved in every trouble spot, but where major national interests or commitments are at stake we cannot withdraw—or withdraw our support from the United Nations when it is at work in such areas. To do so would only breed whirlwinds of disorder which in time could directly affect our own security.

For all of its grief and difficulty, the Congo has hopeful aspects which must not be forgotten. Its millions of citizens now have their destiny in their own hands. Their new freedom may for a time mean merely freedom to mismanage their own affairs. But that too can be educational. It is possible and even probable that 20 years from now the Congo will have found its own road to peace and progress. On that day the potential riches of the country will begin to contribute to the well-being of the Congolese people, all of Africa and the world.

Arthur Herzog, in *The New York Times Magazine,* tells of a Belgian employe of the Congo River Boat Company who commented on Congolese events following independence. "Before," he said, "there were 1,100 Belgians with the company. Only 130 now remain. The Congolese are the bosses now. A year ago I thought the boats must stop running altogether. Perhaps they are a little less clean, perhaps there are more delays, shortages of equipment, aggravations; but they run. That's the important thing; they run."

In time too, if the world gives it a chance, the Congo will also run.

VIII

The Tortured South

Across the waist of Africa today, like a jagged scar, is the borderline—or, rather, the battleline—between black Africa and white Africa.

From its easternmost point on the Indian Ocean the fateful line moves west along the border between the Portuguese colony of Mozambique on the south and independent Tanzania to the north. At Lake Nyasa, still following the Mozambique frontier, it snakes southward under newly independent Malawi and turns again westward until it meets the Zambezi River at the border of Rhodesia. Thence it follows the great river upstream between white-controlled Rhodesia to the south and newly independent, black-controlled Zambia to the north. Upon reaching Victoria Falls and the eastern edge of the vast Portuguese colony of Angola, the line turns northward and windingly moves between Angola and the Congo until, at its westernmost terminus, it plunges into the Atlantic Ocean.

On a map of Africa it is a twisting line. In our lives, however, it is the moving edge of history. To its north are the independent black nations of Africa, most of them born since World War II. To its south are eight countries that at this moment are still controlled by white minorities. The forward march of independence and self-rule has been stopped at these outposts—perhaps momentarily, perhaps for some time to come. To a large extent, politically they remain in the 19th century, although under siege by all the revolutionary ideas and forces of the 20th century.

Like electricity gathering in the atmosphere before a violent storm, great and potentially dangerous forces are now forming on both sides of the battle-line. The independent states to the north are increasingly insistent in their demand that colonialism and white domination of black populations be swept totally from the vast African continent. And southward of the line, likewise, the cords of tension grow more taut. Black African political movements have begun to take shape—some of them new and feeble, others already organized for protest and, if necessary, for sabotage. Increasingly the whites in every area feel a sense of challenge if not of fear. Everywhere in the region the rumble of independence from the north has been heard, and the day of the showdown grows closer.

The first "revolutionary" leader from southern Africa I ever met was Chief Albert Luthuli from the Republic of South Africa. The year was 1948. He had come to the United States under the sponsorship of a church group and I met him at a reception in Washington, D.C. I remember his quiet, modest manner and the fact that everything he said reflected his deeply religious background, acquired in missionary schools in his home country.

The next time I saw him was in Oslo, Norway, in 1961, where he had come to receive the Nobel Peace Prize. He was permitted by the South African government to make the journey only because the pressure of world opinion had been so great; until his departure—and after his return—he was confined to his little farm in Natal Province. He was forbidden to engage in any kind of political activity. He could not even move from his home without special police permission.

Over the years his appearance and manner had grown only more dignified and impressive. But his approach to the problem of freeing his people from white injustice had remained much the same. "I have spent more than 30 years of my life," he told me, "patiently and politely knocking at a closed and barred door. I am not discouraged, but the question now must be faced whether patience and politeness alone can ever bring results."

Young revolutionary leaders whom I have since met are impatient, less inclined to believe that non-violent methods will enable them to break the grip of white control in their countries. One such is Holden Roberto, leader of a revolutionary move-ment in the large Portuguese colony Angola. He is a slender, intense person in his early forties who com-pleted his high-school training in the adjoining country of the Congo. He speaks good French as well as Portuguese and passable English. "But Portugal understands nothing but the language of gunfire," he once said in my office. "We want to be reasonable, but if they refuse to be, then we are prepared to fight. And we will take guns and sup-plies from any country willing to give them."

Another such leader, Dr. Eduardo Mondelane, is head of the liberation forces of the second great Por-tuguese colony in Africa, Mozambique. He too is a young man; his wife is an American girl; he ob-tained a Ph.D. at Northwestern University in Illinois and then left a university teaching post in the United States to take command of his political movement in East Africa in 1963. When I saw him at his small busy headquarters in the city of Dar es Salaam, Tan-zania, he said: "Most of all we need more well-educated young men. It is virtually impossible for any black boy to get even a decent high-school education in Mozambique. But we also need soldiers. I am sorry to say it—but the only road to the negotiating table with Portugal crosses through the battlefield."

If Mozambique does become a battlefield, it will be because 66,000 whites in that country insist on keeping control over the lives of 5,650,000 non-white Africans.

If Angola is split by revolution, it will be because 215,000 whites exercise full, harsh power over 4.6 million non-white Africans.

If Chief Luthuli's country, the Republic of South Africa, is someday plunged further into a bloodbath, it will be because in that unhappy country 3.3 million whites hold 13.8 million non-white Africans in serfdom.

The chart shows more of this arithmetic of white control in the other parts of southern Africa. The figures add up to instability and danger, to political crisis that at any moment can explode. If it does, the tremors and repercussions may reach every part of the globe, for modern weapons and millions of people will be involved.

Politically the crucial fact about such an eventuality is that the fighting that will occur will be between blacks and whites, and it will take place in a context of the blacks fighting in the name of the broad moral and political principles that have powered human events throughout this century—self-determination, democracy, human rights and racial equality.

For the United States the problems of southern Africa present especially painful choices, because our nation is the symbol and the leader on the side of such political ideas. We are also wrestling with serious racial problems within our own country, and two of our European allies, Great Britain and Portugal, are deeply involved in the area.

If tension and fighting become worse in southern Africa, it is inevitable that other international forces will be drawn in. The independent African countries to the north will play an ever larger role in the struggle. Russia and China will, for political and propaganda reasons, become involved. And the United States, even if it wished, could not remain aloof. Thus the problems of southern Africa are not a local affair; a bloody riot in a suburb of Salisbury or Johannesburg will be felt almost instantly in Lagos and Addis Ababa, London and Washington, Moscow and Peking.

The region of southern Africa today consists of eight countries, different from one another in many respects, and uniform in only one—the fact of political control by a white minority.

Starting at the dividing line between independent Africa to the north and southern Africa, let us examine the different areas one by one to judge their prospects for political change, racial justice and stability.

ANGOLA AND MOZAMBIQUE

A look at a map of Africa will show that Angola and Mozambique form a kind of gateway to the south. If Portugal and the white settlers of these areas can suppress African revolt and maintain their political control, then the rate of political change in all the countries to the south will be slowed down. But if the black populations of Angola and Mozambique can gain power, then the tide of African nationalism will quickly reach the boundaries of the Republic of South Africa itself, the final stronghold of white supremacy.

Portugal is a small and poor European country that, a few centuries ago, was a great world power. She has never forgotten those days of glory, even though she has now lost almost all of her colonial empire with the exception of Angola and Mozambique. For Portuguese pride as well as for the Portuguese economy, these two African areas are therefore especially important possessions.

It is a curious fact that Portugal as a colonial power has spoken of her "mission" in the colonies in high-flown terms—yet her actual practices in dealing with the inhabitants have been unusually harsh.

Thus, she sees herself as carrying what was formerly known as the "white man's burden" in attempting to civilize and Christianize the African. Dr. Antonio de Oliveira Salazar, who has headed the Portuguese government for 30 years, has said, "As a nation, we are the trustees of a sacred heritage; we consider that it is our duty, and in the interest of the West, to safeguard it, and we sacrifice ourselves by fulfilling that duty. . . ."

Portuguese practices of slavery in times past, and of forced labor in more recent years, have produced repeated outcry from humanitarian groups in various parts of the world. Prior to World War I the world was scandalized by reports from the island of Sao Tome off the coast of East Africa. Over a period of 30 years, 70,000 to 100,000 Angolan natives were brought from the interior of Angola in chains and sent off to work in the cocoa plantations of the island. Such was the brutality of treatment that although the work contract was for five years, not one single worker was ever known to have returned home.

Until very recent years living conditions for the Africans in the Portuguese colonies were as bad as could be found anywhere in Africa and educational opportunities were minimal. At the same time Portuguese policy was not racist in the sense of maintaining an absolute color bar against African advancement. Any African who somehow managed to become educated and to reach "civilized" standards, as defined by the Portuguese, could become an *assimilado* and achieve legal equality with a white Portuguese citizen. But until certain reforms were instituted in 1961 the number who actually achieved this status was extremely small: *less than one-half of one per cent of the total African population.* The policy of racial tolerance of Portugal has been described by Dr. Salazar in these words: ". . . Because it was in a multi-racial type of society that we constituted ourselves eight centuries ago . . . we have been left with a natural inclination . . . for contact with other peoples. These contacts have never involved the slightest idea of superiority or racial discrimination."

Until 1961 Portugal herself maintained the illusion that her native populations in Africa were bound to the mother country with strong feelings of love and sympathy. Indeed, she had been able to persuade much of the world that the Africans in her colonies were more interested in being Portuguese than in becoming independent.

On February 4, 1961, however, the Portuguese self-delusion about conditions in her colonies fell apart. On that night several hundred Africans in Luanda, the Angolan capital, stormed the police barracks. In the rioting that followed, 24 Africans were killed, 100 were wounded and another 100 were arrested. No sooner had the disorders in Luanda been suppressed than the northern part of the country exploded in scenes of terror. In the following months several hundred whites and many thousands of Africans were killed.

Conditions in the colonies were at least momentarily openly exposed to world view, despite the most active Portuguese efforts to rebuild a propaganda screen around them. The Portuguese government hastily attempted to institute certain reforms. Nevertheless, in succeeding months the revolutionary movements of both Angola and Mozambique were rapidly strengthened. The Angolan movement used the Congo as its operation base and began to train a guerilla army. The Mozambican movement under Dr. Mondelane set up its headquarters in Dar es Salaam in Tanganyika (now Tanzania). In 1962 and 1963 these groups grew in strength, and in Angola a considerable part of the country was actually seized and held by rebel forces.

At the United Nations the African and Asian states intensified their pressure on Portugal and a series of critical resolutions was passed in the General Assembly. The United States—which at first was reluctant openly to criticize Portugal, an ally in the North Atlantic Treaty Organization—nevertheless finally joined the critics of Portuguese policy.

Portugal made some token changes in the face of world opinion. Minimum wage standards and minimum working ages for minors were instituted and the practice of forced labor, but not contract labor, was finally abandoned. However, Portugal mounted a costly and vigorous military effort to drive the rebels back in Angola and to seal off the borders between Mozambique and Tanganyika. Moreover, within the two colonies the Portuguese secret police, called the PIDE, ruthlessly suppressed all African political activity.

On the whole the Portuguese efforts to repress the rebels have been successful. The rebel-held regions of Angola were recaptured and minor forays of the Mozambican rebels have been repulsed. Consequently the two rebel organizations, in frustration, have begun to break up in quarreling factions. And the leaders, in growing bitterness, have begun to turn to the Communist countries, particularly to China, with requests for military and financial help.

The situation is therefore stalemated. How long the stalemate can continue is difficult to predict. If chaos again occurs in the Congo, if disorder spreads in the other adjoining independent African states, and if Portugal can maintain the expense of a continuing major military effort, then the rebels will have extreme difficulty in advancing their cause. But if the Portuguese program of repression falters, or if the rebels should attain major military support from the African or the Communist states in the future, then the situation could change radically. One thing at least is certain: if the African people of Angola and Mozambique should capture political control of the two areas in the next few years, it will be extremely difficult to prevent two more Congo-like situations from developing. For Portugal has left the native populations so pathetically and almost totally unprepared for self-government that extraordinary measures of technical and educational assistance are urgently called for.

RHODESIA

Toward the end of the 19th century the history of the landlocked interior of southern Africa was profoundly affected by the genius and eccentricity of a legendary Englishman, Cecil Rhodes.

A sickly boy, son of an English parson, he had moved to South Africa to regain his health. But he became in the course of time one of the wealthiest men in the world by his control of South Africa's great diamond-mining industry. Subsequently his holdings and interests extended to gold after rich deposits of the Witwatersrand were uncovered in the eighteen-nineties.

Turning his attention northward, he then persuaded the British government to grant his British South Africa Company virtually a free hand to take control of and exploit the minerals of the territory stretching north from Bechuanaland across the Zambezi and east to Portuguese Mozambique.

The chief of the Matabele tribe, which inhabited the area, was Lobengula, a large and intensely black man, usually naked except for a kilt of monkey skins. He agreed to turn over to Rhodes's company exclusive rights to the minerals of the area in return for the promise of £100 per month plus 1,000 rifles and a steamboat with "guns suitable for defensive purposes."

As things turned out, Lobengula was finally driven from his own country—one of a long list of African chiefs who over the centuries attempted to make agreements with the white men, only to lose everything in the end.

After a long period of friction and bickering, fighting finally broke out between the Matabele and the newly arrived settlers. Sick and discouraged after a series of defeats, Lobengula made a final attempt to salvage his situation. He put all the gold sovereigns he had received from Cecil Rhodes in a bag and sent them back, naïvely thinking that if he gave the white men back their gold they would give him back his country. "White men, I am conquered. Take this and go back," his last message said.

Ever since, the black man has been in a subordinate position in Rhodesia. But there are many important contrasts between the situation in Rhodesia and that in the Portuguese colonies to the east and west. In Rhodesia the black man's labor has been used but not brutally exploited. His educational opportunities in Rhodesia have been less restricted, and in recent years a constitution has been adopted which in principle permits certain Africans to vote and even to sit in the Rhodesian Parliament.

Since 1923 Rhodesia has been largely—but not totally—self-governing. Great Britain still has certain limited powers over Rhodesian legislation and must give her approval before basic constitutional changes can be made. Great Britain has insisted, for example, that before she will accord full independence to Rhodesia she must be convinced that all parts of the population, including the Africans, have been consulted and are basically in agreement with the removal of her political control.

Even though the white settlers have talked of "political partnership" with the Africans, a rigid social and color bar has been maintained. Throughout Rhodesia, I have seen signs reminiscent of Jim Crow conditions in the American South—signs over lavatories, drinking fountains and waiting rooms sharply segregating the races.

The enormous social and psychological distance between the whites and the blacks was brought home to me vividly after a recent visit to one of the native reserves, or tribal areas, of Rhodesia. There I had seen toothless old men and rickety children and great numbers of skinny cattle scrabbling for bits of grass on the dry earth.

But at the entrance to the airport, when I went to

my plane to leave the country, there was a large
plaster dog on its hind legs, holding a little cup between its front paws. On the dog was a sign reading
PLEASE LEAVE YOUR COINS FOR THE WELL-BEING OF
OUR PETS and signed by the local Society for the
Prevention of Cruelty to Animals. It struck me as
quaint, sentimental, Victorian—and about as far re-
moved from the acute needs and concerns of the Africans in Rhodesia as anything that could be imagined.

Frank Clements, ex-mayor of Salisbury—the
beautiful modern city that is the capital of Rhodesia—has rather accurately described the general
attitude of the whites toward the Africans in these
words: "The European is not opposed to African social and economic advancement. . . . He has not,
however, been able to accept the African's conten-
tion that advancement is inexorably linked with the
exercise of political power."

And it is precisely on this point that race relations
in this country have broken down. To many of the
whites the concessions offered to the Africans have
seemed great and generous; but to the Africans they
have seemed both too little and too late.

The whites have watched with increasing fear and
apprehension the rebellion in Angola, upheavals in
the Congo, and the spread of one-party government
in independent Africa to the north. Increasingly
they have come to feel that the preservation of

"European standards and civilization" requires a slowing down, if not a backing up, on political concessions to the Africans.

On the other hand, the Africans, watching the acquisition of political power by black majorities in the countries to the north, and seeing independence and majority rule achieved by the adjacent countries of Zambia and Malawi, which were formerly jointed with Rhodesia in the Central African Federation, have become only more impatient for political control.

The tragedy is that in this pleasant country, which only a few years ago seemed to be on the road to a peaceful and stable multi-racial society, racial hostility is increasing. The white government is moving away from a liberal course, and what had seemed to be a flexible evolutionary situation now seems to be increasingly rigid and explosive.

Some of the whites are demanding complete independence from Britain so that they can deal with the native problem in their "own way"—meaning probably the indefinite postponement of African political advancement. The Africans, increasingly bitter, are demanding immediate and outright political control; and Great Britain, using the limited power available to her, is attempting to bring the conflicting parties into negotiation, but without much success.

THE SATELLITES OF SOUTH AFRICA

Moving farther southward, we encounter four particularly primitive and impoverished areas, all of which are heavily under the influence, if not the control, of the powerful economy of the Republic of South Africa.

Three of these are fragments of land, remnants of Britiain's former colonial empire in Africa. They are the so-called High Commission Territories of Bechuanaland, Swaziland and Basutoland. Queen Victoria once called them "mere fleas in my blanket."

Bechuanaland, the largest of the three, is a vast and sparsely populated tableland. Almost two-thirds of it consists of the Kalahari Desert, which is the last refuge of the aboriginal Bushmen. Swaziland is a tiny area tucked in between the Republic of South Africa and Mozambique. Relatively rich in soil fertility and mineral resources, the country is governed by the conservative Paramount Chief of the Swazis and a small group of enterprising whites, who control most of the industry and own much of the land of the country.

Basutoland, the third of the High Commission Territories, is a mountainous little island of territory entirely surrounded by the Republic of South Africa. The scenery is as beautiful as Switzerland's, but the people are extremely poor because overgrazing has denuded much of the highlands of grass and has led to serious erosion in the arable land below.

All three of the areas are intimately connected, economically, with the Republic of South Africa.

Bechuanaland sends most of its modest exports of beef, agricultural products and minerals to the Republic and also depends on it for the employment of some 20 per cent of Bechuanaland's able-bodied workers. Swaziland exports two-thirds of its products to South Africa, and some 10,000 Swazi men work in the South African mines and industries as migrant laborers. Basutoland exports its wool, mohair and a few agricultural products to South Africa, and at any given time roughly two-thirds of its able-bodied men are at work in South Africa. Most of the cash income of the territory derives from money they send home to their families.

Britain somewhat reluctantly accepted jurisdiction over the three territories in the latter half of the 19th century in order to block German and Boer ambitions in southern Africa, to regulate tribal disorders and to protect the tribes, at their request, from incursions of white settlers in the neighboring areas.

For many years it was assumed that they would be eventually incorporated into South Africa itself. But because of racial policies in the Republic of South Africa, Britain finally rejected this possibility. Instead she has responded to demands for self-government and independence of the territories, and they are now well on their way to this objective. Before 1968 all three should become independent countries.

However, though they may fly their own flags and have their own representatives at the United Nations, the weakness and the poverty of the three territories will leave them under the strong influence of—if not at the mercy of—the Republic of South Africa.

SOUTH-WEST AFRICA

In the southwest corner of Africa, adjacent to the Republic of South Africa, is the large but little-known country of South-West Africa. It is about the size of Texas, with a population only slightly exceeding half a million. The land is largely arid, but the mineral resources are rich and commercial fishing along the coast is highly profitable.

This primitive area became a German colony in the late 19th century at a time when the European countries were madly scrambling for colonies in Africa. The severity of German rule is suggested by the story of the Herero tribe, which revolted against German rule in 1904. In suppressing the revolt the German authorities killed 65,000 of the 80,000 members of the tribe and deprived the remainder permanently of their land and possessions.

After World War I, South Africa hoped to annex the territory, but this demand was refused by the victorious Allied Powers. Subsequently South Africa accepted a League of Nations mandate to administer the territory and promised to "promote to the utmost the material and moral well-being and the social progress of the inhabitants of the territory. . . ."

Immediately afterward, however, the country was thrown open by South Africa to white settlers and hundreds of large farms were allocated to incoming whites. The Africans were limited to native reserves in 1922 and racial segregation was progressively applied thereafter. Several of the tribes have attempted to revolt, but punitive expeditions by South Africa have broken their resistance.

Since the demise of the League of Nations and the creation of the United Nations in 1945 the status of South-West Africa has been somewhat ambiguous. South Africa has refused to place it under the trusteeship system of the United Nations, but, on the other hand, has not attempted simply to annex and incorporate the country.

Two African states, Ethiopia and Liberia, which were members of the old League of Nations, have now brought suit against the Republic of South Africa before the International Court of Justice, contending that South Africa by her racial policies has failed to fulfill her duty to promote the well-being of the inhabitants of South-West Africa. The court's decision is expected in late 1965. If it decides that South Africa has in fact failed to fulfill her obligations, a critical and difficult situation could develop. At that point the Afro-Asian majority in the United Nations could demand the removal of South African authority over the area. They might call for its independence or for direct United Nations supervision.

From the viewpoint of South Africa, however, South-West Africa is extremely important, both economically and strategically. It can be expected, therefore, that South Africa will resist vigorously any attempt to take the territory from under her control. Thus the South-West Africa case may become an important test of the authority of the United Nations and of the World Court. And the intervention of these international influences may in time accelerate the political evolution of this extremely backward country.

Thus, among these various areas, some—such as Mozambique and Angola—are rock-solid in the determination of their white minorities to resist African political control. Some—such as the so-called High Commission Territories—are in full and rapid movement toward independence. And two—Rhodesia and South-West Africa—are in ambiguous transition. In this complex picture of rigidity and change the emerging forces of history are constantly at work.

Someone has said that southern Africa resembles a child's top in shape. If so, the steel-shod tip on which it gyrates is the Republic of South Africa. If balance is lost in the Republic of South Africa, all else will falter and fall. But as of today—on the very brink of disaster—it continues steadily to spin.

	Non-Whites	Whites	Ratio
Angola	4,600,000	215,000	21-1
Mozambique	5,650,000	66,000	85-1
Rhodesia	3,800,000	224,000	17-1
Basutoland	700,000	2,000	350-1
Swaziland	272,000	10,000	27-1
Bechuanaland	346,000	4,000	86-1
South-West Africa	500,000	73,000	6-1
South Africa	13,800,000	3,300,000	4-1

IX

South Africa—Riches and Racism

SOUTH AFRICA, lying at the southernmost tip of the continent, is a country of magnificent scenery and climate, richly endowed with natural resources and currently enjoying a robust economic boom. The future for this country and its 17 million inhabitants should be bright indeed. But because 13.8 million of them are non-whites and 3.3 million are white, and because of the insistence of the whites on the economic, social and political subordination of the blacks, reasonable relationships between the races have broken down. As a result the future of South Africa is dark with uncertainty and quite possibly smeared with blood.

South Africa was originally settled some 300

years ago by the Dutch, who wanted to establish at the Cape of Good Hope a provisioning station for their ships at the halfway point between Europe and the Orient. In the first century and a half after the settlement of Capetown the Afrikaners, as the colonists of Dutch origin came to be called, gradually moved toward the interior, encountering and fighting various African tribes on the way. The second 150 years of Afrikaner history was one of struggle against the English settlers who had occupied the Cape after the Napoleonic Wars. The conflict between the two groups led to the Boer War of 1899-1902, as a result of which the Afrikaners were forced into an uneasy partnership with the British in the new Union of South Africa. But strong resentments remained; and after World War II the Afrikaners finally succeeded in taking political control of the country. They promptly broke its ties with the British Commonwealth.

In the years since they have controlled the country the Afrikaner Nationalist Party has made apartheid—pronounced "apart-hate," and meaning a policy of "separate development of the races"—the law of the land.

But to separate the races economically, socially or physically in South Africa is to attempt to separate scrambled eggs. Sixty per cent of the blacks actually live and work in so-called "white" areas, and more and more are being attracted to such areas from the native reserves by the prospect of industrial jobs.

Under the theory of apartheid the African is offered a measure of self-government only on the reserves, which are called "Bantustans." Some 40 per cent of the black population lives in these Bantustans, which consist of only 13 per cent of the total area of the country. The black man, or Bantu, is permitted to live in the "white" areas only so long as he is employed. And even if he lives continuously in such an area for years he is regarded as a "temporary resident," a visitor almost completely without legal rights. The key defect of apartheid is that it gives no dignity and no hope to the urban Africans —who are at the same time the most numerous, educated and politically active part of the African population.

Politically the African outside the Bantustans cannot vote in national or provincial elections; he cannot serve in Parliament. Nor can he advocate political, industrial, social or economic change, even by picketing or other peaceful action. Similarly, his basic human and social rights have been destroyed. His movement is strictly regulated by the Pass Laws and his right to remain in any white area is subject to the most extreme and arbitrary requirements. He is limited to specified residential areas and to separate and inferior schools, hospitals and public accomodations.

The human meaning of these restrictions is often tragic. One recent case in the city of Capetown is typical of thousands of others. The African maid of a white family, who had lived in the city nine years, got married and lost her job. Without a job, she lost her permission to remain in a "white area" and was forcibly put on a train to return to the place from which she had originally come, called Kimberly. There her only connection was that many years before she had lived with a sick uncle, who had since died. She had no relations in Kimberly, no home to go to, no job. Her marriage, one month old, was subjected to indefinite separation from her husband, who would lose his job if he were to leave Capetown to join his wife.

The African's economic rights have likewise been made meaningless. In the rural areas he is effectively reduced to serfdom by laws that make it a criminal offense for any African farm laborer to leave his employment without the written permission of his employer. In the cities he cannot, as a worker, bargain collectively, participate in a strike or aspire to the higher and more remunerative positions that have been reserved for whites. In actuality some of these restrictions are occasionally not applied because of the government's economic needs, more often they are. In any event, by the terms of the laws and regulations, the black South African has been reduced to a mere commodity in an economy based on virtual slavery.

Again the human meaning of the regulations is sometimes heartbreaking. Oliver Tambo, an African political leader has put this forcefully: " 'Abantwana balala ngendlala!' This is the anguished but all too familiar cry of a starving mother in South Africa's reserves, writing to her husband, telling him that the children are starving. He is working on a white farm, in competition with convict labor, or he is in a mine receiving wages far below those enjoyed by white miners, or maybe he is sweeping the streets of some city and earning £3 a week, from which he pays for his food, rent, train or bus fare to and from work, wherever he may be working. If he sends any money, it is all spent within a few days of its receipt. His wife writes a second letter reporting how many of the children are ill, and a third one telling which of them has already died. But, precisely because the children are starving and dying of starvation, he must remain working. He must find work and accept any wage."

The South African government has quite understandably found it necessary to enforce apartheid against growing discontent, and its methods have become more and more ruthless and degrading. South Africans, both black and white, are now effectively deprived of due process of law. When detained under certain charges they cannot seek legal advice or have recourse to the courts. They may be arrested by any police officer without warrant and in the past they have been "legally detained" for an unlimited succession of 90-day periods without notification of lawyer or family.

The International Commission of Jurists, commenting on the South African Sabotage Act of 1962, said that the bill reduced the liberty of the citizen "to a degree not surpassed by the most extreme dictatorships of the left or right. This measure is a culmination of a determined and ruthless attempt to enforce the doctrine of apartheid and is not worthy of a civilized jurisprudence."

As a result of its racial policies South Africa has now brought down upon its head a more nearly unanimous condemnation by world opinion than has any other government in modern times or perhaps ever in history. Not even in the case of Hitler Germany or Stalinist Russia has the world so united in expressing its moral disapproval. However, in the face of such condemnation the South African government has not shifted its policy in any degree and has only become more defiant.

The adamant stand of the government has left the large majority of the country's population of nonwhites with no outlet for their discontent other than violence. For the past 40 years the political organizations of the non-whites in South Africa have been devoted to principles of non-violence. This, however, is now changing. Chief Albert Luthuli, the

Nobel Peace Prize winner and a long-time advocate of non-violence, said after the sentencing of a number of African leaders to life imprisonment in 1964: ". . . in the face of the uncompromising white refusal to abandon a policy which denies the African and other oppressed South Africans their rightful heritage—freedom—no one can blame brave just men for seeking justice by the use of violent methods; nor could they be blamed if they tried to create an organized force in order to ultimately establish peace and racial harmony."

As a result, incidents of planned sabotage and mass terror have become increasingly frequent since 1962. To deal with such dangers and to break up the underground organizations that have been formed, the South African government has moved vigorously to impose penalties of various kinds and of varying severity upon any participant in any protest action.

The South African police are well organized, armed with the most modern equipment, rigorously disciplined and thoroughly versed in anti-sabotage techniques. They are a highly mobile force, with a strength of 30,000 men, equipped with riot trucks, armored cars, dogs, tear gas and automatic weapons. The regular force is supported by a reserve understood to number 6,000 men. It has a sizable political branch empowered to open mail, tap telephones and search houses at any time. Particular stress has been given in recent months to the development of an informer net in non-white areas and it is believed that this internal spy system is now highly effective.

Total government expenditures for defense and police have tripled in the last three years, from $112 million in 1960-61 to a requested $362 million for 1964-65. In its presentation to the Parliament the government stressed its intention to train every white youth from the age of 17 to fight. Thousands of other whites will be organized as *"Kommandos"* who will have rifles and emergency rations in their homes and farms so they can take up arms at a moment's notice. White women's self-protection clubs have been formed, and a new kind of brassière now on sale features a pocket in which a small pistol can be concealed.

Whether sabotage action and terrorism will be able to paralyze the life of the country or whether government police and military forces will be able to control any violent protest remains to be seen. But the tragedy is that this country of rich potential is at war with itself, that the complete breakdown of race relationships jeopardizes all that has been developed in the past and all which might be achieved in the future.

As the outside world views the simmering situation, many are filled with deep anxiety and many proposals are heard in favor of some form of outside intervention to break the impasse. Some are concerned primarily about the immorality and injustice of what is being done to the blacks. There are those who feel that the longer the situation brews, the more violent and damaging will be the outburst of fighting when it comes and the greater will be the dangers to world peace. As a result, various nations at the United Nations—through increasingly severe and increasingly specific resolutions—have attempted to exert pressure on the South African government. The independent African states, through their Organization of African Unity, have not only denounced South Africa but are trying to impose some form of economic boycott, a difficult matter given the great economic strength of South Africa and the relative economic weakness of many of the members of the O.A.U. The Communist powers, both the Soviet Union and China, are watching the South African situation with interest because of its enormous propaganda importance, and both countries have markedly increased their programs for the training of political refugees from South Africa in political, agitational and military techniques.

On balance, however, it does not seem likely that any or all of these efforts at intervention can be decisive. First of all, many persons and many governments doubt the appropriateness if not the legality of intervention by the world community in the "internal" affairs of a sovereign state—even when these internal affairs have dangerous and inflammatory external effects. But, assuming agreement can be reached on some form of international intervention, great practical obstacles will remain. Effective economic sanctions against South Africa will be extremely hard to organize and enforce—and in addition they might have the effect of hardening, not improving, the internal political situation. The independent African states by themselves probably do not have the power to inflict any serious damage or pressure on South Africa. Communist efforts to encourage and support saboteurs may have some small effect, but it is extremely unlikely, given the massive defense preparations of South Africa, that such violence supported from the outside can seriously endanger the Afrikaner government.

As a result, it now seems likely that the situation in South Africa will simply fester for some time to come, spreading its poison more and more widely, until the problems of other countries of southern Africa are resolved. But a sudden outburst is not impossible—as occurred in the killings at the town of Sharpville in 1960. If such an eruption should occur, it is certain that the reaction of much of the world would be extremely strong, for South Africa is now an explosive issue for the emotions and the conscience of the world.

As did slavery in the 19th century and Nazism in the first half of the 20th century, the issue of human and political rights for the black majorities of southern Africa now poses ultimate choices for nations as well as individuals—choices whose consequences for good or evil will ripple outward to the ends of the world and resound for generations.

X

The Tigers Beyond the Gates

"AN INDEPENDENT NATION has to have an army," one African leader remarked to me not long ago, "just as a gentleman has to have a necktie."

Most of the new African states now maintain military forces. Ten nations have "armies" of 1,000 men or less. At least seven, however, have more than 10,000 men each in their organized combat and policing groups. It would be pleasant to think of all these as "neckties"—as status symbols, as armies that will parade but not go to war. Yet Africa's history is one of invasion from outside the continent and dissension within, and neither of these perils is absent in the Africa of the mid-nineteen-sixties. There are tigers beyond the gates, and not all is peaceful within.

Tensions exist between the newly independent states for reasons that are sadly familiar to mankind: conflicts over territory, differences in race and religion, different views of future goals and the ways to attain them. Africa is divided today along several lines—between Arab states and Negro states, between moderates and radicals, between French-speaking and English-speaking groups. Too, there are memories of bloody tribal wars and the sad inheritance of a jumble of borders. And there still lingers, in some of the new nations, the atmosphere that prevailed in the days when independence was won: a revolutionary attitude, a certain recklessness and antagonism toward all symbols of authority and control.

Africa is one of the battlefields on which the cold war is being fought, and on this continent, as elsewhere, the Soviet Union and Communist China are involved in their own competition. Wherever the giant powers face one another, there is peril; whenever the giant powers are poised, one against the other, tiny sparks can ignite great conflagrations.

The threat of such sparks exists. For example:

¶The Democratic Republic of the Congo has charged before the United Nations that certain sister African countries have been undermining it, inspiring and aiding rebellion within its territory, and doing everything they could to make it impossible for that state to exist as a free, sovereign, independent nation.

¶The President of Upper Volta has accused the President of neighboring Ghana of sending subversives to neighboring countries and of attempting to impose "arbitrary socialism" on the rest of Africa. He has said further that unless Mr. Nkrumah of Ghana "altered his hostile attitude," Upper Volta might cut off the water for a new Ghana dam.

¶The Foreign Minister of Senegal has said, "There is a kind of 'internal imperialism' in Africa. Some of the states here seem even to want to impose their own regimes on all of Africa."

¶Some of the Arab states of North Africa have become particularly divisive. After seven long years of bloody war against France, Algeria is bitter and radical; she has openly fomented violence not only against the white minority regimes in the south, but also against moderate African governments that do not support her approach. Egypt, under General Nasser, has sought greater influence in Africa; if she gains it, one immediate benefit for Egypt will be greater support within the United Nations for her crusade against Israel—more votes, more political allies. She has therefore been willing to stir trouble within any African country where a change in leadership would suit her purposes.

To date, the splits and disagreements have mostly

been verbal. But the words could in time be replaced by bullets. Some farsighted African leaders
recognize this threat, realizing that if African nation
fights African nation, then all hopes for progress
and freedom are diminished. They have called for a
spirit of unity and Pan-Africanism, and out of this
spirit they have built the Organization for African
Unity, the O.A.U.

The O.A.U. is new. Yet in settling an ugly border
dispute between Algeria and Morocco, it showed
that it could become a useful mechanism for peace.
And by initiating a number of cooperative development projects it has demonstrated that it may become a valuable instrument for economic growth.
To the degree it grows stronger, the threat of self-
destruction for newly independent Africa will grow
weaker.

In any case, even more dangerous are the power-
ful forces that may intervene from beyond the
shores of the continent: the Communist states of the
Soviet Union and China, the countries of Western
Europe and, some Africans would say, the United
States of America.

The world Communist movement has had a long-
standing interest in the underdeveloped countries,
and Africa is no exception. According to Peking
and Moscow, the victory of Communism in the new
states could have an important bearing on the influence of Communism in the industrially advanced

countries of the West. Consequently by a variety of means—propaganda, subversion and economic and military assistance—both the Soviet Union and China have tried to spread their influence in Africa.

The Soviet Union moved quickly in the wake of independence to give economic assistance to the new African nations, but their first efforts frequently ended in failure due to Russian ineptness and heavy-handedness. Along the runway of the airport in Accra, Ghana, a row of Ilyushin turbo-prop airliners stood idle for many months, their engines hooded. After purchasing them from Russia, Ghana quickly realized that they were uneconomical to operate. Thereafter they stood as a monument to the first and unsuccessful phase of Russian economic efforts in Africa.

China, on the other hand, began by trying to win diplomatic recognition from the African states, and in this effort she has had dramatic success. Of the 36 independent nations, 18 now maintain formal relations with Communist China.

In late 1963 Chou En-lai—accompanied by a 60-man entourage—spent 53 days visiting 10 African countries—the most extensive tour of Africa ever made by the prime minister of a major power. At the end of his visit he said, "An excellent revolutionary situation exists in Africa. That is why it must be in the forefront of our attention." Thereafter China began to make larger grants of economic aid. She became directly involved in revolutionary activities in some of the independent states. She expanded her training programs for young political leaders from the white-controlled southern areas.

To some degree Soviet and Chinese aims in Africa coincide. They both want to discredit the Western countries, to break ties between them and the African states, and to dramatize Communist sympathy with anticolonialism. But in equally important degree they are in conflict.

The Chinese representatives in Africa, in capital after capital, denounce the Russians in terms as strong as those they use against the United States. They call Russia "imperialistic" and "exploitative"; they scorn her as "reactionary" and "indifferent to the struggles of the African against colonialism"; they stress that China, as a poor nation herself, understands best the problems of impoverished Africa; and they hammer on the fact that Russia, like the United States, is white—while China, like Africa, is not.

On the other hand, Russia cannot allow the Chinese to appear more radical or sympathetic to the African than herself. And so, although the Chinese and Soviet programs in Africa are separate and in conflict, the one will tend to set the pace for the other, and Africa is likely to be the scene of increasing Communist activity—to the dismay, let it be said, of many of Africa's leaders, who watch with foreboding this growing struggle between the titans of the Communist world on their continent. In the summer of 1965, shortly after Premier Chou En-lai made a second visit to Africa, I visited Kenya and talked with President Jomo Kenyatta and several of his ministers. Most were blisteringly critical of Communist tactics, especially those of the Chinese. How deeply will the Soviets and the Chinese commit themselves to winning Africa? How effectively will the Africans be able to contain and protect themselves from that struggle? The answers to these questions lie in the future—and will help shape the future.

THE UNITED STATES

To the eyes of Africans, the United States is one of the great outside forces whose intervention could be helpful—but could also spell danger. Similarly, African feelings about the role which the United States has so far played in the liberation and the development of the continent are both friendly and bitter.

As many Africans see it, the part played by the United States in their struggle against colonialism has been an unheroic one. During the 19th century, after American independence from England had been won, the United States spoke out repeatedly against foreign imperialism in Africa. During World

War I the idealism of President Woodrow Wilson and his advocacy of "self-determination for all peoples" gave the United States great prestige among the few African leaders who were then already working for the liberation of their homelands. Again in 1946, at the San Francisco conference establishing the United Nations, we spoke out strongly in behalf of self-determination and of the U.N. Trusteeship system.

But shortly thereafter the cold war broke out and rapidly intensified. What little interest the United States had developed in African independence was pushed into the background because of urgent and dangerous problems of maintaining world peace. The Soviet Union under Stalin—as soon as the war against the Nazis and the Japanese had ended—moved quickly to seize control of Eastern Europe, to extend Russian influence in the Middle East and Asia, and to threaten the security of the devastated countries of western Europe. In response, the immense strength of the United States was pressed into an urgent effort to rebuild our own military power and to help rebuild European productivity and unity. During this period, when Africa did fleetingly receive American attention, it was largely in the form of sympathetic words in behalf of self-determination. On concrete issues—when, for example, a dispute involved an African colony and one of our European allies—the United States sided with Europe.

From America's viewpoint, the policy of these years was in the main successful. The Soviet challenge was thrown back. Peace was preserved. Europe was rebuilt. But the reaction of Africans to our policy and priorities ranged from disappointment to resentment.

"The United States is not a wicked nation, but only a spineless one," said one African leader. "As far as I am concerned, there is no longer any deep bond of friendship and affection between my people and yours. In the moment of our crisis, we feel, you turned your back on us and let us down. This is something that a nation, like a man, never forgets."

Such African judgments may seem harsh and unfair—and they are in no sense universal, for there remains much good will toward the United States in Africa and real appreciation of the assistance we have provided. But such critical feelings do exist and must be understood, for they form the background of many explosive and extreme African reactions to recent events.

Ironically enough, not only are many Africans sharply critical of the United States but some of the white settlers in Africa, the former masters, are equally vehement. A Kenya farmer, originally from Britain, denounced the United States in my presence. "America has been more dangerous in Africa than Communism," he said. "The so-called 'wind of change' would never have begun to blow except for the pious democratic nonsense that has constantly gushed from the United States. You have always sided with the African against the white. Any rascal was your favorite as long as he was black. I deeply resent the fact that your country helped ruin me and all the other whites in Africa."

The violence of such statements reflects the powerful feelings, on both sides, of the fight for independence in Africa. They also show that even the bystander in any dispute may be the target for the fears and frustrations of both combatants. Yet the policy of a great power such as the United States cannot be guided by a desire for popularity; it must seek to achieve the more important aims of justice and stability—even though the immediate rewards may be largely in the form of criticism.

THE INFLUENCE OF WESTERN EUROPE

The countries of Western Europe, the third major external source of influence upon Africa, present special and important dangers and opportunities.

Some of the former colonial powers of Europe have sometimes shown an inclination after their departure from Africa to reenter the scene, thereby causing great disquiet and suspicion among Afri-

cans. Belgian troops landing at Elizabethville in the
Congo, French troops landing in Gabon to reinstate
a deposed government, and the invasion of Egypt by
the British and French at the time of the Suez crisis
in 1956 are three examples of such action.

However, in many of the new nations of Africa
there is today great and growing involvement with
the former colonial masters—and clear evidence of
friendly feeling. Although political control has been
broken, there remain innumerable strong ties—cultural, economic, personal—between Africa and Europe.

Moreover, these ties may in the future greatly increase, with results that need not be harmful and
could be of enormous benefit to the independent
African countries. Already the European countries
are providing major financial support to the new
African states and European business firms have a
deep interest in independent Africa. Western Europe is in the midst of a sustained economic boom
and the new power of Europe is beginning to radiate
outward to other parts of the world in quest of markets, sources of supply and commercial arrange-
ments of all kinds. Africa, on the other hand, needs
capital and special skills, and the great resources of
Europe are not only the most familiar but are also
the closest at hand.

It seems possible, therefore, that one of the important developments of the coming years may be

greatly expanded relations between Europe and Africa. Such a development may be ominous in the view of some, and may even suggest the "recolonialization" of Africa in new and more subtle form. But if it can be built on the basis of partnership, of realism and mutual respect, then the result could be a tremendous gain for the hopes of development in Africa and stability in the world. Even more important would be the possibility of an eventual triangle of cooperation and mutual interest between Africa, Europe and the United States.

THE UNITED NATIONS

The last of the list of external factors important to the future of Africa—and the most benign—is the United Nations.

To date, this strange and wonderful political creation has been of precious advantage to Africa. It has given force to the ideas and intangible factors which have accelerated the independence of the continent. By its peacekeeping efforts the U.N. has protected the new states from some of the destructive impact of outside forces to which they might have been subjected. It has given them a forum for the expression of their hopes and concerns, and an influence in world affairs despite their lack of economic or military strength. Through its economic, social and educational programs the U.N. has also provided them with major help in their development —help all the more welcome because it did not present the threat of direct foreign influence or control.

For the African states, therefore, it is gravely disquieting that the United Nations has recently fallen into serious difficulties. Africa is not primarily responsible for these difficulties; they result largely from deep discord among the great powers. But the Africans have contributed to the problem by their sometimes excessive demands upon the organization and by their inexperienced and impatient behavior.

For the peace of the world, as well as for the well-being of the African states, it is essential that the United Nations successfully find its way through its present crisis. With all the dangers the new African states face—from other nations of Africa itself and from the great powers waiting and watching from outside the boundaries of the continent—the destruction of the effectiveness of the United Nations would dangerously undercut their chances for progress and even survival.

For some time to come, African independence will depend on the presence of a buffer and friend, such as the United Nations, and on international respect for the rights of small nations. Without the United Nations the potential violence of the world —if ever unleashed—could crush the fragile independence of Africa like an eggshell.

XI

The Awakening Giant

THIS, THEN, is Africa today—vast, varied and contradictory, an awakening giant shaking off the sleep of centuries and bursting with promise and danger. Its emergence is one of the events of our lifetime—along with the discoveries in nuclear science, the political tranformation of China and the birth of the United Nations—that may alter human history for centuries to come.

It is therefore a new and major fact in our lives—a fact we now must accept, live with and attempt to understand. We in America have been deeply affected by all that has happened in the recent African past, both the good and the evil. But what is now most urgent is to look to the future: How will the new nations of Africa alter our lives? What attitude should we take toward them? How can we build healthy, friendly relationships between our two continents? What form of assistance should the United States now give the independent African countries? What actions should we take with regard to the southern areas not yet independent?

Perhaps the first step is for each continent to learn more about the other. Until now the African has known the Britisher or the Frenchman or the Portuguese or the Arab. For him, the American has seemed unreal—but probably very rich. One young African boy wrote to the African-American Institute in appreciation for a scholarship he had been given to attend high school in his own country. "I am ineffably gratified to receive this kindness from your fat country. . . ."

Great as the ignorance of the African about the American may be, the American's ignorance of Africa is no less. And his indifference is even greater. Even in the U.S. Congress there is little interest or awareness. In the House of Representatives a handful of members show some knowledge and concern. But in the Senate there is as yet not a single spokesman for active American cooperation with the new Africa.

So now must begin the long, slow process by which one continent enters the consciousness of another. Information will have to filter slowly into the textbooks and the school curricula; into the minds of teachers, editors, politicians; and then into the awareness of average citizens. Only then will Americans and Africans be able to think of each other not as two-dimensional caricatures but as real people struggling with real problems. Only then will the United States be to the African more than newspaper headlines about racial battles in Alabama and Los Angeles, pictures of skyscrapers and the sight of a tourist rushing down the road in a giant automobile. Only then will Africa become for the Americans more than stories of political outbreaks and jokes about cannibalism and witch doctors.

But beyond knowledge there must develop understanding. Repeatedly over the centuries Africa has been invaded and raped by the outsider. The African's values have been despised, his history obliterated and his person abused. His blackness was made a badge of shame. In the deepest reaches of his heart this heritage has produced self-doubt and resentment. His most profound desire is to reestablish his dignity as an independent person.

Much that now seems irrational or oversensitive or hostile in Africa today comes from centuries of hurt to pride and dignity. At times African leaders have given voice to a kind of race hate toward whites as repugnant as that which has often been hurled at the blacks—but such occasional racism by Africans reveals most of all the depths of their old resentments. Americans will make perhaps their finest contribution to the future of our relations with Africa by understanding the personal and powerful connection between race and independence for every African.

As in any new acquaintance, both Africans and Americans must make positive efforts to contribute to their new relationships—by changing certain practices and attitudes and by concrete acts of cooperation.

On the African side, it will be helpful when the banners and the slogans of the independence struggles are finally put away and the African settles down and relaxes in his new condition—when he is sufficiently secure in it to no longer feel obliged to flaunt it constantly in the face of others; when the shrill tone of righteousness leaves his voice; and when he becomes a partner with whom ordinary conversation and ordinary friendly disagreement becomes possible.

We can be encouraged. Increasingly, the African is realistic and flexible in his dealings with the non-African, and increasingly self-confident. In an amazingly short time Africans have junked a large part of the emotional baggage that accompanied their efforts to oust the foreign colonialists and have come to grips with the practical problems of running their affairs, earning their living and getting along in a world full of mischief and danger. With amazing speed, too, the Africans have acquired the skills and habits of sovereign nationhood. At the United Nations five years ago they had trouble finding the delegates' restaurant. Today they are the masters of the political and diplomatic intricacies of the organization.

Now the African must learn that politics is more than a game. Kwame Nkrumah's advice, "Seek ye first the political kingdom and all else shall be added unto you," was probably sound during the process of liberation from colonialism. But now that independence has been achieved, political maneuvering, endless political palaver and obsession with the preservation of personal political power are not effective means for dealing with the knotty problems of nation-building and of economic and social progress. The African quite possibly has a natural genius for politics and it may be doubly difficult, therefore, for him to resist overindulgence in it.

The most costly obstacle to effective relations between Africa and the Western world, however, is the tendency of some African leaders to continue to reflect the mentality of colonialism. They still tend to blame their troubles on others, consciously or unconsciously assuming that the solution of their difficulties is somehow the responsibility of others. In the words of one prominent African leader (of whom this mentality is not characteristic), "All of us have acquired the bad habit of speaking of the enemies of Africa as 'colonialism,' 'neo-colonialism' and the cold war. But too few of us recognize that these are really phrases that only help us escape from our own responsibility. It is much easier to blame one's problems on some devil of the past than to face the problems of the present . . . easier to scold real or imaginary devils from abroad than to cope with difficulties at home. The real enemies of independent Africa today are our own ignorance and lack of skill, our own selfishness and irresponsibility, and our own loyalties to family and tribe rather than to the whole nation."

African leaders are no more given to escapism and nonsense than leaders elsewhere. But the needs of their countries are especially urgent. Many of the most grievous blocks to progress in Africa are internal and home-grown and can be dealt with only by Africans themselves. In some countries it is the waste and extravagance of the highest officials; in others it is rampant corruption among the governing elite; and in still others it is a massive problem of drunkenness on the part of a good portion of the ordinary population.

The more quickly African leaders devote themselves to the correction of such faults and recognize the mote in their own eye, the more quickly will they win the sympathy and support of their own populations and, incidentally, of the United States as well.

For Americans, the adjustments of attitude that will be required for effective partnership with Africa are even more numerous and fundamental.

We must develop a sense of perspective. Partly because of our unfamiliarity with Africa and partly because of the dramatic events of recent years, American reactions have swung like a pendulum from one extreme to another. The first wave of independence in Africa produced great excitement and optimism in the United States; but a few months later disorders and the trend toward one-party states led to exaggerated pessimism about African prospects. Even now news of a Russian diplomatic maneuver in Brazzaville or of a shipment of Chinese arms to Zanzibar tends to produce sweeping predictions about a Communist takeover of the continent; and the gory details of some minor tribal battle instantly arouses American doubts about African civilization.

For Americans to begin to see such daily developments and fragments of information in some perspective will require considerably more knowledge of African society, history and political institutions than most of us possess today. A greater awareness of our own history and of the slow emergence of our own national unity and political stability would also help.

By the clock of American history Africa is now in the seventeen-nineties. That was the period when our young nation physically drove out of the country and into Canada a good portion of those who had opposed the Revolution, tarred-and-feathered many who remained, and expropriated (legally and illegally) their property. We oppressed the native tribes, saw corruption flourish in our new officialdom and denounced the idea of foreign military bases on our soil.

We took large quantities of foreign aid and credits, simultaneously denouncing the greed of those who offered them. We applauded every revolution anywhere, declared our firm intention to remain neutral and aloof from the struggles among the then Great Powers, and issued holier-than-thou statements on the political and international troubles of other nations.

We passed the Alien and Sedition Acts, which made it a criminal offense to organize to oppose measures of the Government or even to speak ill of the Congress or the President. The Jeffersonians complained bitterly that the Federalists had created a one-party state and were resorting to illegal measures to smash all political opposition.

Seen against the broad canvas of history, recent events in Africa, however strange and puzzling, are part of a consistent human pattern. The violence, difficulties and stupidities are no greater than, and little different from, those which have occurred at many other times and places. Nor should it be overlooked that Africa is also manifesting the same noble idealism and determination that other peoples have shown and which, in the end, have generally produced economic and political progress.

It is particularly important—but it will be particularly difficult—for Americans to erase from their minds prejudices or preconceptions about Africa and the black man. In all the curious and distorted history we have learned in school, the African when mentioned at all has always been a "native" and his country somebody's colony or dependency. The cultural achievements and the past civilizations of Africa have been neglected or belittled, and we have unconsciously accepted the judgment of Western moralists and missionaries that the African's customs and beliefs are inferior.

The influence of such misinformation, ignorance and bias on our present political attitude toward Africa is subtle but powerful. Even now it is difficult for us and for some of our leaders to think of the Africans as anything but children. We tend almost unconsciously to expect "obedience" from them; we feel most comfortable in the role of teacher to them; and we are easily exasperated by their assertiveness, which we tend to regard as "talking back"—as misbehavior.

For most Americans, seeing Africa objectively is additionally difficult because we are a nation in profound conflict (as well as transition) in our attitude toward Negroes in our own country—both in the North and in the South. In our reactions to reports of events in Africa there is doubtless some tendency to project upon that scene the conceptions or prejudices that stem from our own feelings about race problems at home. With remarkable inconsistency we both disparage the potentialities of American Negroes and of Africans and at the same time expect superhuman achievements from them.

As John Steinbeck, the novelist, recently said, "I am constantly amazed at the qualities we expect in Negroes. No race has ever offered another such high regard; we expect Negroes to be wiser than we are, more tolerant than we are, braver, more dignified than we, more self-controlled and self-disciplined. We even demand more talent from them than from ourselves. A Negro must be ten times more gifted than a white to receive equal recognition. . . . We expect Negroes to be more courteous, more gallant, more proud, more steadfast. In a word, while maintaining that Negroes are inferior to us, by our unquestioning faith in them we prove our conviction that they are superior."

This same contradiction is discernible in the reactions of Americans to Africa. How marvelously we honor Africans by expecting them, despite their poverty, their illiteracy, their decades of experience with life under colonialism and their inexperience in handling their affairs, to be able to produce full-blown democracies and measurable social and economic progress in a handful of years!

But here again the basic trends are hopeful. The status of the Negro in American life is changing and the racial attitudes of many Americans, particularly of younger people, are moving rapidly away from the prejudices of the past. Moreover, the American Negro community itself, though understandably preoccupied with problems of civil rights at home, has shown increasing interest in African affairs. In the future the presence of an important Negro element in American life will come to be understood as a valuable element in our own democracy—and as a powerful factor in the development of warm and strong relationships between the United States and Africa.

The contradictions in our attitudes toward Africa are reflected in some of our policies. President John F. Kennedy once said to Africa and the other underdeveloped areas: "To those people in the huts and villages of half the globe struggling to break the bonds of mass misery, we pledge our best efforts to help them help themselves for whatever period is required—not because the Communists may be doing it but because it is right." But the United States in its governmental assistance puts Africa at the bottom of the list of continents which receive our help. Moreover, the flow of American private charity to Africa is extremely limited. As a nation we spend more each year on potato chips than we do on aid to the largest of the impoverished continents.

Yet there are a good many Americans who believe that the United States should reduce even further its assistance to Africa. They argue that because Africa is not geographically adjacent to the powerful Communist countries or close to our own shores, it is strategically of little importance. They claim that the United States is already trying to do "too much for too many" and should therefore leave Africa essentially to the help of the countries of Western Europe.

The same kind of problem is presented by the not-yet-independent southern areas of the continent. There, too, considerations of moral principle clash with short-run economic and military concerns. To date, the United States has attempted to resolve its foreign-policy dilemma by issuing statements and declarations in behalf of racial justice and majority rule without backing up our words with action. Thus, in the case of the Republic of South Africa, American representatives have repeatedly expressed our official disapproval of apartheid, but until very recently no official action has been taken even to impede the movement of U.S. private investment into South African industries. Yet the profits from these are largely derived from the use of exploited African labor.

President Lyndon Johnson recently said: "We may well be living in the time foretold many years ago when it was said: 'I call heaven and earth to record this day against you, that I have set before you life and death, blessing and cursing: Therefore choose life, that both thou and thy seed may live.' This generation of the world must choose: destroy or build, kill or aid, hate or understand."

In Africa, as elsewhere, such choices must be made —and they must be made in terms both of national interest and of national principle. For what is wise on moral or humane grounds is likely in the long run to prove wise in terms of national security.

If we neglect the needs of the independent African countries for development, our neglect could lead to political and strategic dangers to ourselves and the whole world. Failure on our part to help bring about racial and political justice in southern Africa could deeply corrode the influence and world leadership of the United States. The issues there touch directly on the basic ideas and ideals upon which the American political system and society have been built and upon which our prestige as a world leader rests. Moreover, the problems of race —in addition to its spiritual importance—has a direct bearing on the prospects for world peace. The Secretary General of the United Nations, Mr. U Thant, has said, "There is the clear prospect that racial conflict, if we cannot curb and, finally, eliminate it, will grow into a destructive monster compared to which the religious or ideological conflicts of the past and present will seem like small family quarrels."

The African continent is, in an important way, a testing ground for many of the new and important ideas of the modern world—self-determination, human rights, human equality and the possibility of progress in regions which have stagnated and been suppressed for centuries.

If Africa can find stability and progress and dignity in the years to come—and if the United States gives her full measure of help—we will have enriched our lives, served our own most precious values and helped ensure our own and the world's survival.

We will have helped conquer a frontier a thousand times more difficult and more important than landing on the moon.

INDEX

WALDEMAR A. NIELSEN

Waldemar A. Nielsen brings to the study of international affairs a background of extraordinary breadth as scholar, diplomat and administrator. A Rhodes Scholar and research scientist before World War II, he became a naval officer after Pearl Harbor.

Following the war, he dealt with problems of international trade as a State Department official. In 1947 and 1948, as Special Assistant to the Secretary of Commerce, he was one of the small group of economists and diplomats who formulated the Marshall Plan and later he held a high diplomatic post in its Paris headquarters. In 1949 and 1950 he participated in the planning and launching of the North Atlantic Treaty Organization.

In 1952 Mr. Nielsen returned to the United States to join the Ford Foundation, where he was responsible for its social science programs and European activities. In 1960 he headed the staff of a White House Commission to study U.S. information, cultural and educational activities overseas.

Since 1961 Mr. Nielsen has been President of the African-American Institute, the largest U.S. private organization concerned with African development and African-American relations. For the past two years he has served as chairman of a Council on Foreign Relations study group on southern Africa. A frequent contributor to *The New York Times Magazine,* he has written extensively for national publications. His book *African Battleline* was published in 1965.